# CALIFORNIA UTOPIANISM

# CALIFORNIA UTOPIANISM

## Contemplations of Eden

## Robert V. Hine

series editors:

CALIFORNIA UTOPIANISM:
CONTEMPLATIONS OF EDEN
*Robert V. Hine*

Manufactured in the United States of America.

Library of Congress catalog card number: 81-66063

ISBN 0-87835-115-9

1 2 3 4 5 · 5 4 3 2 1

# EDITORS' INTRODUCTION

MENTION THE NAME CALIFORNIA and the popular mind conjures up images of romance and adventure of the sort that prompted the Spaniards in the 1540s to name the locale after a legendary Amazon queen. State of mind no less than geographic entity, California has become a popular image of a wonderful land of easy wealth, better health, pleasant living, and unlimited opportunities. While this has been true for some, for others it has been a land of disillusionment, and for too many it has become a place of crowded cities, congested roadways, smog, noise, racial unrest, and other problems. Still, the romantic image has persisted to make California the most populated state in the Union and the home of more newcomers each year than came during the first three hundred years following discovery by Europeans.

For most of its history California has been shrouded in mystery, better known for its terrain than for its settlers—first the Indians who arrived at least 11,000 years ago and then the Spaniards who followed in 1769. Spaniards, Mexicans, and blacks added only slightly to the non-Indian population until the American conquest of 1846 ushered in an era of unparalleled growth. With the discovery of gold, the building of the transcontinental railroad, and the development of crops and cities, people in massive numbers from all parts of the world began to inhabit the region. Thus California became a land of newcomers where a rich mixture of cultures pervades.

Fact and fiction are intertwined so well into the state's traditions and folklore that they are sometimes difficult to separate. But close scrutiny reveals that the people of California have made many solid contributions in land and water use, conservation of resources, politics, education, transportation, labor organization, literature, architectural styles, and learning to live with people of different cultural and ethnic heritages. These contributions, as well as those instances when Californians performed less admirably, are woven into the design of the Golden

State Series. The volumes in the Series are meant to be suggestive rather than exhaustive, interpretive rather than definitive. They invite the general public, the student, the scholar, and the teacher to read them not only for digested materials from a wide range of recent scholarship, but also for some new insights and ways of perceiving old problems. The Series, we trust, will be only the beginning of each reader's inquiry into the past of a state rich in historical excitement and significant in its impact on the nation.

Norris Hundley, jr.
John A. Schutz

# CONTENTS

# PREFACE

**T**HERE ARE PEOPLE into whose heads it never enters to conceive of any better state of society than that which now exists," wrote Henry George in 1879.[1] This judgment about his fellow man stood in contrast with his own hopes for equality and abundance for the workingman, for an end to land monopolization, and for controls on corporate power. As an economist, George had rationally analyzed these concerns; but as the "prophet of San Francisco" he was assumed to be more than a rationalist, more the visionary utopian. His practical side dwelt in the present; his utopian bent ranged across its true home, the future.

Katherine Tingley, California's preeminent theosophist, frequently trained her eye on that same future. She once told of unburdening her utopian soul to John Charles Frémont: "In a golden land, far away, by the blue Pacific, I thought as a child that I could fashion a city and bring the people of all countries together and have the youth taught how to live and how to become true and strong and noble and forceful warriors for humanity."[2] She was then in New York talking with Frémont, who suggested that she investigate Point Loma as a locale in which to realize her childhood dream. She did, and there just north of San Diego her fantasy was translated into aquamarine glass domes, Greek theaters, flowering groves, and schools for children of all ages from a variety of nations.

Her pathfinder, Frémont, was something of a dreamer, too, but he imagined steaming locomotives, pictures of growth and American expansion, not the advent of a radically changed society. Tingley and George shared with him the practicality and even hard-headed realism of builders, but they went beyond him in foreseeing qualitatively different worlds, fresh Edens. It should not be forgotten, however, that Utopia is often rooted in reality. On the spectrum between impracticality and attainability, it is a movable point, partaking of both. In its tendency toward one it is never devoid of the other.

California as a state of mind has been heavily weighted with utopian idealism. Though the mood may be hard to identify as prevailing or dominant, it has certainly been unusual, even remarkable. Like William Wordsworth's mystical Nature, Utopia has been deeply interfused with California. One can hardly imagine utopians like Henry George or Katherine Tingley evolving as they did in any other intellectual climate.

Since utopia ramifies so widely, I have been heavily indebted to colleagues in other areas of study. In literature my thanks go to George Knox, Harry Lawton, Marshall Van Deusen, John Ganim, George Slusser, Ernest Callenbach, and Edwin Bingham; in political science, Francis Carney and Melvin Gurtov; in sociology, Mark Gottdiener; in religious history, Edwin Gaustad and Hal Bridges. Don Stoutenborough has read the manuscript with an eye to style. I have profited, particularly in connection with the modern scene, from talking or corresponding with Beth Nelson, Lou Durham, Eric Raimy, Yana Parker, Betty Romanoff, Ramon Sender, and Geoffrey Selth, and from clippings sent over a long period by Robert Chandler and Heidi Putzker.

My gratitude is immense for the assistance of John Spurlock, Edward Mierau, Alan Curl, Raul Robles, Mario Mojarro, Mary Scaff, Allison Hine, Debbie Bode, and Sharon Brock.

I owe much to the staffs of the California Historical Society; the Bancroft Library, Berkeley; and especially the Library of the University of California, Riverside. Susan Lasater and Constance Young have typed cheerfully and skillfully.

The aid and support of Shirley has, as always, been present in every step.

R.V.H.

Riverside and Carlsbad
July 1, 1980

# CHAPTER ONE

# The Spectrum of Prophecy

T HE COASTAL STRIP from San Luis Obispo to Seattle seceded from the United States and proclaimed itself the Republic of Ecotopia. Dedicated to the proposition that all technology should be nonpolluting, it recycled its wastes, prohibited jet planes in its air space, proscribed guns, substituted ritual war games for spectator sports, eliminated the inefficiencies of competition, required only a twenty-hour work week, and decentralized its industry. Its people enjoyed marijuana, dressed fancifully, and expressed their emotions openly. Deaths from air and chemical pollution were memories, whereas the greater United States had been able to reduce those statistics to only thirty thousand dead a year. Ecotopia looked on a place like Santa Barbara, just south of its border, as a kind of Tijuana. America fearfully sealed off Ecotopia from contact, and in American cities such as Reno, Ecotopians were believed to be eccentric outlanders.

Ernest Callenbach, who lives and works in Berkeley, expressed in his Ecotopian vision that shimmering contrast between the ideal society and the critical problems of its parent world. Such a dream was like the graceful, symmetrical little pine tree Mark Twain saw in *Roughing It,* standing amid the hellish fumaroles of a desolate island. Ecotopia, however, was laid on Pacific shores, a terrain that has become almost tritely utopian. And, furthermore, the land was the terminus, the last chance. California after all was a place where, in Joan Didion's words, "the mind is troubled by some buried but ineradicable suspicion that things had better work here, because here, beneath that immense bleached sky, is where we run out of continent."[1]

Utopia in literary guise often takes place in some utterly remote spot, some Edenic distant land where its changes are unimpeded by the established mores. Hence the metaphor of the island or hidden valley from Thomas More to Aldous Huxley. The beginnings of the story are associated with some catastrophe—a shipwreck or political upheaval. Ecotopia, for example, followed a period of inflation, recession, and economic chaos. The Survivalist Party, led by women, took advantage of the conditions, capitalized on the concentrations of science and technology, seized atomic weapons, and trained them on eastern cities. Thus Ecotopia was left alone to free itself from billboards and the worship of economic growth. Fundamental change was accomplished through cataclysm and the product was a transformed socioeconomic environment.

Utopia can also be initiated by a simple move to a new environment. Here the position of California in the nineteenth century—beginning as a foreign land and continuing far removed from the centers of population yet not so isolated as to be forbidding—provided a natural setting. After the 1880s those who came to its mild climate were most often the dupes of wild ballyhoo, but even so the escape to its warmth and freshness proved a compelling context for other change. Refugees from blizzards could in fact watch oranges ripen in the winter, and the All-Year Club never ceased advertising that theme. How many brochures pictured shore waves in February pulsing like diamonds laid on the breast of the world? The captions gloried in valleys and forests rich enough to feed and provide timber for a thousand cities beside blue bays. It was a land to fan the romantic imagination. George Wharton James, the Methodist circuit rider who came to southern California in the early 1880s, called it "a God-like gift," unparalleled in the civilized world.[2] Its Spanish past, its missions and ranchos, would be romanticized into a utopian memory, and an exaggerated grandeur would likewise clothe its future.

Yet lotus eaters and other dwellers in paradise do not necessarily become pilgrims of perfection. The native Californians may have enjoyed their environment but did not seem to coax from it any further ideal. Indian society drew no imaginary blueprint nor voiced a manifesto. It was devoid of the linear expectations of dramatic upheaval followed by substantial change, and filled instead with ceremonies of annual renewal, a sense of cycle, a yearning for origins carried in ancient traditions through the generations.

The Spaniards were, of course, cut of different cloth. They named California for the pearly sands of a romantic novel, but that alone did not make them utopian. They sought the northern shores primarily to extend an empire or to advance the sway of the Cross. Cabrillo and Ulloa may have raced for golden cities or dreamed of fantastic inland waterways, but they were direct servants of the imperial and commercial designs of their homeland. They would frame no utopias out of the raw California material.

Utopians, unlike Indians or Spaniards, see their environment as a painter might conceive his canvas or a sculptor his stone— the implicit embryo of a new creation. There came to be a breed of Yankees who thought of California in these terms. They carried with them the restless images of change. True, after 1848, most Yankee eyes, like the Spanish, also smarted from hopes for golden commercial advantage, imagining steaming locomotives, clanging trolleys, bustling harbors, and flowing aqueducts. Few of these people were utopian, because they were as much extensions of existing society as were the Spaniards building their presidios and missions.

There is an unrealistic strain, a wistful, dreamy quality, in utopia, and this its scoffers frequently emphasize. Wishful thinking or exaggeration, however, do not alone make utopia. The early explorers were sometimes magnificent exaggerators. In the seventeenth century Sebastián Viscaíno and Juan Torquemada described Monterey Bay as calmly protected from all winds, and Antonio de la Ascención reported beaches of pearl and mountains of gold. But such unreality was not followed by any social implications. John Sutter, on the other hand, dreamed of his own empire, dramatically compensating for his pre-California failures through a transforming vision. Sutter's utopia, with its fields and vassals, mills and halls, was more complete than that of most immigrants. George Donner and his party, for example, expected a better life in California, but their dream was rather closely linked to their former Illinois farm, perhaps with more sun and flowers, but not high on the scale of unrealistic utopianism.

Expectations of improved conditions, the flying buttresses of utopianism, assumed various forms and functions. Panaceas appealed especially to the retired and the elderly. Railroads and land booms ushered in economic growth that encouraged even higher expectations. People and governments glimpsed a glorious future. But this vision was most often steeped in private property, in the single-family house with its patch of lawn, in the teenager's roaring automobile—all so well described by James Q. Wilson as typical of southern California.[3] It is hard to explain how so much visionary radicalism emerged from this culture of private expectations.

In California the backdrop seemed to encourage more than the simple extension of established ways. There was far more movement in this land the Yankee made, a momentum that was more than earthquakes. It was related to the redefinition of entire environments. It was spun from recurring land booms, peaking in the 1880s and the 1920s. Even barren deserts were to be quickened into oases, like the serious proposals of the 1870s to flood the Colorado Desert, create the Widney Sea, and grow thereby trees the size of sequoias.[4] If this region felt sun as a magnet, steam and gasoline would in time become its gods. But they were worshipped in an aura of fantasy, especially in southern California. Here were the movie sets, the Arab tents, the Greek temples, the Egyptian columns, and the Venetian plazas, the Mediterranean, theatrical whimsies so often expressed in architecture. It was a strange paradise, one gained by human will through the expansive energies of a westering people. These were the backdrops of utopia, not the vision itself, but the context in which it could more easily emerge.

Chiefly on disillusion are the illusions of utopia built. Utopians are like Prometheus on the rock, their livers gnawed by dissatisfactions and then daily renewed by their optimism. In California, for example, a rustic band of Bear Flag rebels grew discontented with Mexican rule and projected a new republic. Ezekial Merritt and William B. Ide may not seem like Prometheans defying Zeus, yet in their own stumbling way their

Moorish whimsy in Southern California: Ocean Park Bathhouse, c. 1900
(*Courtesy of History Division, Los Angeles County Museum of Natural History*)

disillusions and grumblings bore the germs of utopia. One of
their colleagues saw Ide "possessed of many visionary if not
utopian ideas."[5] Ide dreamed of a state in which the virtuous
would not be taxed and in which there would be no compulsory
military or other service. The Bear Flaggers were like many
Yankees, discontented enough with their lots in the East to have
pulled up stakes and moved West. Then they found their promised land several cuts below the promise. But the true utopian,
in contrast with these incipient ones, adds to his outrage a
response which is a challenge, like the raised anarchist's fist, the
fires of hope, the recurring symbols of basic change.

Industrialism and capitalism, associated as they were in the
mind of the young Karl Marx with personal alienation and social
fragmentation, have undoubtedly aggravated most modern utopias. Kaweah's efforts in the 1880s to relocate the socialists and
workingmen of San Francisco was a good example. So, too, was

Upton Sinclair's plan to colonize victims of the Great Depression. They sought fundamental social change, and echoed revolution, even though they tried no direct assaults. If taken seriously, these revolutionary implications were often seen as a threat by the nonutopians. Hence the reaction of derisive laughter or violent denunciation. Upton Sinclair's design provoked such an outcry because its radical connotations were so perceived by established business and agriculture. The utopian is derided as fanatic or lunatic, not an unexpected epithet for the prophet of revolution. Though Marx later in his life disavowed "utopian fantasy," it was a bit as if Christ had denied the prophetic role of John the Baptist. The nonutopian sees utopia as impractical and unrealistic, speculative and hypothetical, enthusiastic and devoid of experience, and so the province of the young. But, as Michael Fellman has pointed out in *The Unbounded Frame,* abstract systems held a peculiar fascination for nineteenth-century Americans. Older inherited forms were thought to be crumbling while newer ones remained undefined. In California, with its imposition of Anglo culture and recurrent waves of migration, settlement, and boom, the assertion was peculiarly apt.

The unrealistic abstractions of utopia, because they might ignore the erratic in human nature and the flux of time, have been seen as static. Arnold Toynbee compared them to arrested civilizations, societies that have lost their drive, too weak to move forward yet strong enough to forestall oblivion. He might have used as examples the California Indians, living in a cyclic culture, unprogressive, with no social mechanisms for change. Inasmuch as individualism thrives in the hurly-burly of innovation, and most utopians have been anti-individualistic, there is some substance to the charge. Further, from the viewpoint of pluralism and growth, it is easy to mistake the utopian craving for homogeneity and common purpose for stasis. Yet if pluralism and growth are found to be chaotic, utopia is the escape to certainty. In its response utopia usually seeks wholeness, the complete integration of the one and the many, and not a diversity of paths.

Toynbee's charges seem unconvincing in the face of the revolutionary implications of utopianism. As Melvin Lasky, editor of *Encounter,* has written in *Utopia and Revolution,* utopia is not an

escape but a manifesto.[6] It is the blueprint of the destination
but does not seriously chart the route, either before or after the
light of the dream. It creates the outlines of a ship but does not
necessarily undertake the voyages. The course may test the
strength of the hull in unforeseen rough weather, but it may not
be proper to criticize the naval architect for not describing that
course: he can only be held responsible for overlooking the
weaknesses in his craft.

More worrisome are the concerns of humanists. They begin
with the Renaissance and utilitarian credos of human dignity
and freedom. When they look at most utopias, as the philosopher Augustine Castle did in *Walden Two* (1948), they find them
regimented, stifling, and unhumanely efficient. H. G. Wells, no
mean utopian himself, observed this quality as the search for
perfection which runs counter to human inexactitude, the essence of humanity. The efforts to regulate the inexactitudes and
the eccentricities produce the anthill and the germs of ultimate
tyranny. The utopian responds that the ascription is unfair,
making utopia no more than antiutopia, as if one must accept
only Aldous Huxley's world of *Ape and Essence* as the future, not
the state of his *Island*. The utopian aspiration may finally have
to include the disheveled social visions of Jack London in the
Valley of the Moon or Henry Miller in the Big Sur, far from
regimented beehives.

One route to the ideal society has always lain through religion, through the ethical demands of faith and the mystical
insights of the initiated. Thus the Sermon on the Mount, because it projects a loving and cooperative society far removed
from the competitive world, has prompted countless utopias.
Then, too, the religious millennium, the sudden transformation,
the Second Coming, is a fertile image for utopia, spilling over so
often into secular religions like Marxism. But for religion absolute freedom is absolute obedience, and through this avenue
comes once more the darker side of utoia. Hence emerge the
wildly distorted, charismatic utopias of Thomas Lake Harris or
Jim Jones in northern California and Guyana.

Josiah Royce may have understood the religious model of
utopia as well as any other Californian. His devout, God-fearing
mother instilled a spiritual bent in her son. She allowed no other
children within their Grass Valley house: it was a symbolic

refuge from the materialism of the Gold Rush. As a student at
the fledgling University of California, writing for the campus
newspaper, he noted the role of ideas behind the events of
history, and would later decry the spirit of the Gold Rush to be
all those qualities abhorred by his mother—greed, restlessness,
opportunism. In 1882 he was invited by his friend William
James to teach philosophy at Harvard University, and the rest of
his life was centered in Cambridge. Yet he played the part of a
roughneck westerner, at least in dress, while at the same time he
was irritated by the romantic interpretations of his home state
such as those of Bret Harte. In Royce's *California, A Study of the
American Character* (1886), he was frank in facing the spiritual
burdens with which the modern state was born. Against the
ambition and avarice, irresponsible freedom and moral elas-
ticity, he painted the pre-conquest Mexicans as a humane,
tender-hearted, proud, and "comparatively guiltless people."

Royce's ideal society was implied in almost all of his subsequent work, especially in the *Philosophy of Loyalty* (1908) and
*The Hope of the Great Community* (1916). The society which
California with all others must struggle to find would be rooted
in strong local attachments, "wise provincialism," the kind of
communal organization once inspired by St. Paul among the
early Christians. In such genuine community "the social group
may show itself wiser than any of its individuals."

These small, limited communities on which the larger nationalism should be built would be training grounds for morality and
social reform. Such provincialism would glorify the local past, as
Royce had done for California, and would be the "saving
power" to remedy the evils of mobility, cultural uniformity, and
interpersonal divisiveness. In Royce's ideal, individual happi-
ness came through cooperative self-surrender to the needs of
the whole. Throughout his life, in the words of his biographer,
Royce was "an unregenerate idealist in both the philosophical
and the popular senses." In California history he found a social
parable full of utopian meaning—the degradation of the present
wishfully to be escaped, and the vision of a radically changed
future, the hopes for which are rooted in the same present.[7]

Royce's utopianism was visionary and imaginative, theoretical
and speculative, impractical, idealistic, even impossible. His
great community, like Alfred Tennyson's federation of the

world, lay on the verge of a social horizon. The position implied, if it did not spell out, utilitarian action. True, other thinkers, such as Aldous Huxley and Henry George, would be more precise and detailed. Yet their utopianism would share a grandness of outline, an expectation of a march toward an unbroken skyline, and a contemplation of California as Eden.

# Imaginative Utopia: From Harte to Huxley

IKE A STERILE DESERT unfit for human habitation—that was the way Lewis Mumford saw the classic literary utopias. They were not only standardized, regimented, and potentially militaristic, but by ignoring human diversity they left little room for fantasy and liberating creativity. "As dull as mud," they could hardly move men to rally in their cause.[1]

This myopic view held a measure of validity, but it overlooked the social aspiration which the genre contained. We have already seen how Ernest Callenbach's utopian novel captured the environmental preoccupation of our time. Likewise we will find how Aldous Huxley's *Island* projected a mix of socialism and mysticism suggestive of the 1960s. If Californians have held a lively and optimistic sense of an ideal society, then imaginative literature written in the state should reveal it.

California produced no full-scale utopian novels until after World War II. Even then the optimistic utopian voices were drowned by visions of a frightful future, the antiutopia, the dystopia, the cacotopia—not the ideal society but a stifling and oppressive one. They deliberately portrayed what Mumford found only implicit in the earlier ideal visions. They stood in the Orwellian nightmare tradition of Huxley's *Brave New World*

(1932), written before he came to Los Angeles. In California George Stewart's *Earth Abides* (1949) and Huxley's *Ape and Essence* (1948) saw a future of holocaust and doom. These were the handmaidens of industrialism, militarism, and environmental destruction that subverted optimism.

Californians historically have worked out their utopias in action rather than in literature. Instead of utopian novels they have set up utopian experiments like Kaweah, or they have proposed utopian programs like Upton Sinclair's EPIC. The utopian novels they have read have been carried from elsewhere, as were *Looking Backward, A Traveler from Altruria,* or *Voyage en Icarie.* California thus became a place where "no place" would materialize into some place.

Still, California literature has embodied many of the separate components of utopian thought—optimism and perfectionism, the implicit revolution, and the millenarian vision. California writers have been quasi or incipient utopians, fellow travelers flirting with the ideas. If nothing else, they have created a state of mind, a context in which the fully developed or activist utopian has felt at home.

In 1854 Francis Bret Harte, then seventeen, came to Gold Rush California. Developing into one of its first American writers, his earliest stories described a past age, life in Spanish California in which he saw "a delicious monotony of simple duties, unbroken by incident or interruption."[2] The setting, however, for which he would always be remembered was the rustic simplicity of a mining camp. In the stories that brought him fame—"The Luck of Roaring Camp," "The Outcasts of Poker Flat," "M'liss," "Tennessee's Partner"—he pictured, not an ideal society, but one that called forth the best in people. The rough Kentuck was transformed through the love of a child and the prostitute starved herself to keep alive the innocent girl. The very air of the camps "induced the wildest exaltations," but red-shirted miners, simple frontiersmen, were serene in their companionship with nature.

This California of Bret Harte was a land of chivalry, a word that he used to mean fraternal bonds. The fraternity was an island society. It was a band of men with gentle courage and boundless confidence in the future. Thus, they listened to utopian echoes of regeneration within a primitive environment allowing no despair over man or his universe.

Harte could represent a line of writers who were positive about human nature as it might be nurtured and glorified in the California setting. George Wharton James, for example, an Englishman who journeyed to America in 1881, ministered to Methodists in Nevada and California for seven years before he suffered a physical breakdown. The air of California and the Southwest restored his health and, through subsequent years of lecturing on the Chautauqua, editing *Out West,* and writing forty volumes about his region, he never forgot the recovery. When he spoke of California, and especially of the Mojave and Colorado deserts, he saw the land refining the soul and rekindling serenity. Writers like Harte and James shared with the utopians a brave sense of fresh beginnings, of clear eyes on clear horizons, of unfolding potential on a new morning.

Benjamin Franklin Norris, like Harte, was brought to California in his teens, that period of one's highest expectations. For a time, when he left California to study art in Paris and when he studied as an undergraduate at the University of California, he was enamored of medieval romances, attracted to a tapestried past redolent of steeds and galleons. Yet for his writing he did not choose the setting of Spanish California, as Harte had once done. Instead, Frank Norris moved away from romance and into the intellectual orbit of Émile Zola. Norris came to accuse the wretched present of scuttling the past and endangering the future. *McTeague* (1889) was a grim picture of San Francisco in which an unloving impostor of a dentist was consumed by greed. *Vandover and the Brute* (1914) portrayed an artist unable to work, driven to gambling, insanity, and collapse. Norris had reached the utopian's dissatisfaction with the world around him.

*The Octopus* (1901) was Norris's stern damnation of forces like the railroad that bound humanity with tentacles of steel. The big San Joaquin landowners, their ranches like manors, legs swung over armchairs as they drank their whiskey, were likewise destructive of the spirit of the small farmer. Such a picture in the hands of Jack London or John Steinbeck would smell of revolution. And one of the characters in *The Octopus,* the saloonkeeper Caraher, occasionally spouted anarchistic rhetoric, but he was ineffectual. The novel claimed no solution, pointed to no golden dawn, only to amoral forces like the growing wheat, cyclic, changeless, eternal.

Two characters in *The Octopus,* however, posed utopian possibilities—Presley, the poet searching for his epic, and Vanamee, the soulful mystic misfit. Presley found his theme in the plight of workingmen, and he dreamed of a society liberated from toil and want. He resorted in the end to violence, but sheepishly and only momentarily.

Vanamee was a more complicated and utopian character, an educated wanderer, tanned, bearded, living in deserts and hills, an alien and a dreamer. He brooded over the death long ago of his Angele. Embracing her grave in the moonlit garden beyond which lay acres of seed-ranch flowers and using his powers of thought transference, he evoked a presence that came to him across the violets and roses. The presence was the maturing daughter by another man of his beloved and in their developing love he saw the victory over death. In the final scenes of the book, the railroad having ruined the ranchers, some of them shot, some of their daughters driven into prostitution, Presley confronted Vanamee for the last time. Vanamee heard the sad details, but watched his young love coming through the sunlit wheat and told Presley that all will work for good in the end. It was the cosmic optimism of the utopian, in this case filtered through the figure of a nature god with mystic auras. As we will see, his type would appear surprisingly often in California history.

Jack London was in the strict sense no more of a utopian novelist than Norris. Yet there are some social visions in London which are not far afield. He was a socialist and for a time signed his name "Yours for the revolution." But his socialism was so much a pose and so inconsistent with his primitivism, as in *Call of the Wild* (1903), that it cannot be taken seriously.

In London's *Valley of the Moon* (1913), however, an idyllic retreat posed an alternative to an oppressive society. Billy, a former prizefighter, and Saxon, his industrious wife, were driven by working-class conditions in Oakland into poverty, drink, and depression. Through the movies, they dreamed of escaping and began three years of wandering, in the process observing how foreigners in agriculture were competing with the pure Anglo-Saxon pioneer stock. Billy and Saxon eventually find their Eden

in the Valley of the Moon in Sonoma County. Billy raised
horses; Saxon, vegetables; and they were so successful that they
found time for thought and culture. Nature was strong and
clean, "like young boys their first time in the ring," said Billy.
Just as Vanamee had concluded, "all the natural world ws right,
and sensible, and beneficent." Knowing this, Californians like
Billy and Saxon "beyond the encircling hills, . . . would find
what they desired."

In London's *Burning Daylight* (1910), Elam Harnish in a raw
Arctic land climbed a starlit mountain and imagined the bleak-
ness below to be swarming with forty thousand men, docks
lined with steamboats, streets solid with cabins and mills and
dance halls. "Whatever he saw, he saw big." In times of despair,
when life for him became "an everlasting funeral procession,"
his visions of the future metropolis would revive him. Back in
California he envisioned Oakland with a hundred thousand
people, teeming docks, efficient ferries, and eucalyptus trees by
the millions.[3] For various reasons Harnish could not profit from
his dream, but such quasi-utopianism would bring happier results for real entrepreneurs like Henry Huntington, Abbott
Kinney, or Harry Chandler.

If Elam Harnish and his kind revolved in a milieu of hopeful-
ness and grand expectations, they enlarged the existing society,
not projecting a new or ideal one. Their optimism, inasmuch as
it suggested commercial speculations, has also been the *bête noire*
of the utopian. Theodore Strong Van Dyke, for example, wrote
of the hills and lagoons of the San Diego hinterland as a virtual
Eden, with fish in stream and sea and marvelous birds still un-
classified. "California has an outdoor charm that will live for-
ever." He was a Princeton-trained Minnesota legislator whose
health had collapsed. Coming to San Diego in 1875, his tall,
handsome, blue-eyed figure became a legend roaming the back
country, restoring his physical fitness. His first book, *Southern
California* (1880), showed the quiet joys he had found.

Ten years later Van Dyke's Elysium had been threatened by
the Elam Harnishes and the boom of the 1880s in southern California. He was appalled at the rapid expansion and haphazard
growth. Fertile farmland was subdivided for profit. In 1890 his
*Millionaires for a Day* was nearly a dystopia in which speculation
converted a bread basket into a roulette wheel in the "greatest

Van Dyke's Elysium threatened by the land boom of the 1880s: San Diego lot sale (*Courtesy of San Diego Historical Society*)

piece of folly that any country has ever seen." As one of his characters, Solomon Sunrise, said of the boom, "We were a lot of very ordinary toads whirled up by a cyclone until we thought we were eagles sailing with our own wings in the topmost dome of heaven."[4]

Writers in California often tried to sail in that topmost dome, especially in colonies of creative culture. While Van Dyke still roamed his San Diego hills, Helena Modjeska, the Polish Sarah Bernhardt, brought to southern California nine countrymen, including Henryk Sienkiewicz, later author of *Quo Vadis*. She had dreamed in her homeland, "Oh, but to cook under the sapphire-blue sky in the land of freedom! . . . nearer to God and better."[5] They settled in 1876 on a farm near Anaheim, and the initial discouragement was deep as they faced their commonplace surroundings. Madame Modjeska stood distraught in the kitchen, trying to satisfy the prima-donna palates. Farm work was vexing; three men were required to kill one turkey. Spirits were high, though, with leitmotifs of Wagner through the afternoons. Sienkiewicz withdrew to a little table under the trees and wrote much of the day. After six months, the intellectuals declared the efforts a financial disaster and sailed for home. But Helena Modjeska stayed behind, eventually captivating audiences and taking her place in the American theater beside Edwin Booth and Otis Skinner.

In 1904 George Sterling and Mary Austin began to attract to
Carmel a loosely organized cultural colony. Their fellows and
visitors included Jack London, Charles Warren Stoddard, Lincoln Steffens, Sinclair Lewis, and William Rose Benét. It was
a Parnassus, sacred to the Muses, but based on developers who
gave artists purchase terms as low as five dollars down and five
dollars a month. Yet Mary Austin said that Jack London and
George Sterling forced them to grapple seriously with issues
like socialism, so the Carmel colony with its simple life and
creative air could perpetuate some sense of social responsibility.

The Carmel colony still existed when Robinson Jeffers at-
tached himself to the region just south of it. From a stone tower
overlooking the sea he observed an outside world as destructive
as that of Van Dyke's speculators. "O from this valley of distress
look up, look back, to Paradise." Jeffers had come to his paradise as a young man. He had wanted to live with his new bride in
Europe, but the outbreak of war in 1914 forced them to look
elsewhere. That fall they rode a coach out of Monterey. "We
looked down through pines and sea-fogs on Carmel Bay, it was
evident that we had come without knowing it to our inevitable
place." For twenty years he lived where his jutting, hand-laid
stone house challenged the ocean and the mists. From his refuge
he dreamed of a better world: "Our children may even ascend
to the stars." "Let us go home to paradise."[6]

Henry Miller came to this same coast in 1944. He already was
acquainted with California. As a young man in 1913 he had left
his native Brooklyn to work and travel in the West. Having read
some Theosophy, he was drawn to Katherine Tingley's Point
Loma colony. But while he was working nearby in San Diego, a
transfiguring influence on his life came in a chance meeting with
Emma Goldman. Her views on anarchy and free love were
critical to all of his subsequent work, beginning with the products of his many years in Paris where he made his name. In 1944
he settled in Big Sur, just south of Carmel, and stayed in those
rugged sea-clad hills until 1961. "This is the California that men
dreamed of years ago," he said, ". . . the earth as the Creator
intended it to look."

Miller wrote of these seventeen years of his life in *The Big Sur
and the Oranges of Hieronymus Bosch* (1958), a rumination on his
personal Walden as well as the people around him, their neigh-
borliness and cooperative ways. The community on the Big Sur

"At one with themselves and all that lives and breathes": Henry Miller and family, Big Sur, 1951 (*Courtesy of Henry Miller and Special Collections, Research Library, University of California, Los Angeles*)

was a collection of refugees from the establishment, people who like Miller had concluded that the outside society was an *Air-Conditioned Nightmare* (1945). They hoped to nurture here a better way. Miller compared the effort to "The Millennium," a painting by Hieronymus Bosch. The fruit on the trees and the creatures below conjured up a time of order and harmony; man was one with nature. The young people of the Big Sur sought a unity. They subsisted on peanut butter and wild mustard greens in order to live in peace. In the process they built an ideal anarchistic community: "the loose, fluid aggregation of individuals who elected to be alone and detached in order to be at one with themselves and all that lives and breathes." Such a community must in time replace the warring, dismembered societies of the world.

Reminiscent of his own flirtation with the Point Loma colony, Miller quoted another California Theosophist, Krishnamurti, who said that in simplifying wants lay the solution of countless social problems. But these Thoreaus of the Big Sur were also living interrelated, cooperative lives, adapting to the ways of their neighbors, if not to their views. Thus they found no inconsistency between their self-concern and what Royce would call the hope of the great community. Near the end of his book Miller fantasized on how that great community might look on the Big Sur one to five hundred years hence. The coast was studded with villas, their broad staircases winding down to the sea and to the boats at anchor. Tables were spread under awnings and wine drunk from golden goblets. There was laughter "rising from thousands of jubilant throats." But there were also, as on the rocky ledges of Greece, chapels and monasteries above the sea. All the people shared and participated in this paradise. Artists were no longer the enemies of society. Instead, they led in understanding man's intimacy with nature and in self-fulfillment. It was a utopia of artistic anarchy with Mediterranean trimmings, a rich blend of hedonism and democracy.[7]

Aldous Huxley first came to Los Angeles in the fall of 1937 while Henry Miller was still in Paris. Huxley's English friend, Gerald Heard, the mystic, had preceded him. As pacifists both men had been disturbed by rising militarism in England. The two took a short auto trip to northern California, stood together in redwood groves, and felt the enveloping stillness renew in them the possibility of peace. As a result of the 1937 visit, Huxley returned the following year to live the rest of his life in southern California.

Huxley's work had taken utopian gambits long before. *Brave New World* (1932) had pictured an efficient future society with complete government planning from the moment of an individual's test-tube conception. It was an antiutopia, smothering thought and creativity. Technology and materialism had run amuck.

*After Many a Summer* (1939) was written partly before and partly after his arrival in California. A millionaire, Jo Stoyte, lived in a villa suggestive of William Randolph Hearst's castle at San Simeon. But through a less affluent neighbor, Bill Propter, Huxley reiterated his dissatisfaction with the hedonistic society. Propter was trying to avoid all entanglements to centralizing power, divorcing himself from utility companies by devising solar machines. He envisioned an economics of consumer and producer cooperatives, functioning in small, self-sufficient towns. But to succeed, the ideal society must be energized by the right kind of people. These should include a fair proportion who in a mystical way "consciously attempt to transcend their humanity." So for Huxley political reform was not in itself sufficient, and any optimism must rest on the transforming of human nature, here and now.

In the foreword to the 1946 edition of *Brave New World,* Huxley offered an alternative to the insanities of his antiutopia. The other possibility would be decentralized or Henry George-ist in economics, humanistic in technology, and Taoist in religion. When in 1948 Huxley again looked at the future in *Ape and Essence,* such an alternative had not prevailed. The novel was an apocalyptic nightmare of Los Angeles following the holocaust of World War III. This loveless society was characterized by human sacrifice and orgy. Far off in the San Joaquin Valley, however, across impassable regions was an isolated community where the older values of love, attachment, and humanity persisted. Conceivably from this withdrawn periphery the regimented horrors of the established society might be cured.

In *Island,* published in 1962, the year before his death, Huxley's utopian ideas culminated. He opened the book with an Aristotelian epigraph that enjoined all utopian thinkers to avoid impossibilities. For Huxley the imaginary country of Pala did deal in realities. It required, for example, isolation to survive, though some worried that its untapped oil resources might attract evil aggressors.

Pala blended the best of East and West. Buddhist ethics and primitive village communism skillfully served the purposes of reason in a cooperative society in which industries were dispersed to suit human needs. Children were raised by Mutual Adoption Clubs in which childhood could involve as many as twenty loving parents in successive homes. Jobs were varied throughout life. Violence and war were countermanded by the yoga of love, springing from the ritual of the moksha, drug-induced sensations which released love and creativity.

The utopia was tinged with sadness, forebodings about the tanks and guns against which it must some day stand. The oil under its land and the subversion of Sears Roebuck catalogues served as Trojan horses. In the final scene the vision was blurred by marching feet and blaring commands.

Still, there was hope in Huxley. In the words of a critic, Christopher Holmes, "*Island* is a final vision of both practical and ultimate truth." Mankind could transcend its present nature. The solution lay in reaching a sufficient number of self-realizations. As for practicality, Huxley, "the scientific mystic" in Hal Bridges's words, could point to his experience with psychedelic drugs beginning in 1953 and his knowledge of utopian experiments. He studied and wrote about the old Llano Colony of socialists in the Antelope Valley. He helped Gerald Heard organize Trabuco, a community intended to bridge East and West, and he wrote the prospectus for the community in 1942. On a stunning slope in the mountains behind Santa Ana, Trabuco invited its members to a simple life, rigid discipline, celibacy, prayer, and study. These were experiments that infused the novel. The dream of Pala was in Huxley's mind as practical as it was visionary, and hence it was truly utopian.[8]

California literature since Huxley, with the notable exception of Ernest Callenbach, has been only peripherally utopian. True, many writers have dwelt on a sordid present and an altered future. Jack Kerouac, Allen Ginsberg, and Lawrence Ferlinghetti rebelled in their private subterranean cultures, while science-fictionists like Ray Bradbury offered future universes. Still, little in their underground worlds or their vaulting space seemed ultimately ideal. Tom Wolfe's *Electric Kool-Aid Acid Test* (1968) might illustrate the approximate level of this utopianism, partial at best. Wolfe recounted the life of Ken Kesey, author of *One Flew Over the Cuckoo's Nest* (1962), who in 1963 settled among the redwoods behind Palo Alto, experimented with LSD, and began to draw followers to his cabin. Fifteen of them, the Merry Pranksters, painted and refitted a bus and toured the country. They were demonstrating a revised life style and a canon of brotherhood. "We're in a period now like St. Paul and the early Christians," Kesey said, a time of beginnings and superheroes. As with St. Paul, he had felt revelations in the lightning: "I pointed to the sky and lightning flashed and all of a sudden I had a second skin. . . ." The power and the direction were reflected in the eyes of the young, especially in the lives of

The experimental mystic: Aldous Huxley, 1959 (*Courtesy of Special Collections, Research Library, University of California, Los Angeles*)

his own Merry Pranksters. "The bus had great possibilities for altering the usual order of things."[9] The exhibition of their shared experience would help change attitudes in others. Psychedelics would pave the way, as with Carlos Castaneda's Don Juan who could see a crack in the cosmos and another reality beyond. The rhetoric revolved around deeper sensibilities, higher consciousness, and the greening of a dawning age.

Wolfe and Kerouac and other quasi-utopians were as expectant of the human potential as Bret Harte had been five generations before. What was missing in their work, if it were to be utopian, was a detailed description of the destination, the plan of the ideal society, the political and economic intricacies, the working models of an Ecotopia or a Pala. Instead they created, like science fiction, "a literature that leads toward a vision of human perfectibility on a collective scale."[10] To practical outsiders, their land may have seemed obscure, but to it utopians would be no strangers.

## CHAPTER THREE

# Attainable Utopia: Political and Economic Visions

THE TRUE UTOPIA demands some radical or revolutionary change. The line, however, between root-and-branch revolution and reforms that do not strike so deeply is sometimes difficult to draw. The dreamer who simply wishes to perfect the present or who is in the process of realizing a whimsy may be on the road to utopia. A planner or real-estate developer, for example, may seek more than profit, imagining his new environment to be liberating for the spirit or reviving lost values. Such melding of the prophet with his profit is hardly unknown. Commodore John Sloat was perfectly sincere in 1846 when he called on Mexicans to accept the American conquest because the attainment of political liberty would be accompanied by a rise in real-estate values. In Sloat's historic wake surged all those frontiersmen who for generations speculated on the promise of expansion. Highways and railroads were often dreams as well as extensions of the marketplace. Yet such expectations were only partly utopian because they did not seek to scrap the basic assumption and start anew.

Two of the greatest nineteenth-century city planners, Fredrick Law Olmsted and Daniel Burnham, combined utopian vision with California reality. Olmsted's first view in 1863 of the countryside around San Francisco repelled him—so many dreary, dry, brown hills. He had already supervised the planning of Central Park in the midst of New York City, and he hoped to inspire similar beautification throughout America. In 1865 a committee from Berkeley hired him to plan a campus for the University of California. Olmsted also helped design Golden Gate Park in San Francisco and later the campus of Stanford University. His ideas looked forward to future needs for recreation in cities, especially for women, and he hoped that such parks would settle the restless, shiftless populations of the West. Lewis Mumford once said that the city was the beginning of utopia, the beginning of hope for the different and changed future. Olmsted foreshadowed this idea to its fullest. It was not surprising that he was friendly with Edward Bellamy, the utopian novelist in Boston, a writer whose work would influence California significantly.

In 1904 an Association for the Improvement and Adornment of San Francisco commissioned Daniel Burnham, designer of Chicago's Columbian Exposition. He used Mediterranean towns for inspiration, then set up a tent studio on Twin Peaks to feel the city as he sketched: "Where the influence about me shall stimulate Golden Gate Thoughts."[1] The resulting plan called for a grand boulevard around the circumference of the city and along the bay. Sweeping diagonal avenues converged on the civic center. Some of the squares were closed to vehicles and one cordon of parks, he prophetically claimed, would be useful in case of fire. The drawings were in the hands of city leaders when the great earthquake and fire of 1906 provided the ideal clearance and opportunity for rebuilding. But Burnham felt himself too old to supervise such a gargantuan task, and the pressures of fast restoration scuttled the implementation of the architectural vision.

Burnham's plan was based among other things on what Kevin Starr calls the Mediterranean analogy: a dream of brilliant, clear light, silver rather than gold, that would in time open California houses with picture windows and glass doors. It was the image that architect George Wyman extracted from the vast airy halls

A dream of brilliant, clear light: Daniel Burnham's "Report on a Plan for San Francisco," 1905; Telegraph Hill, looking east

envisioned in Edward Bellamy's *Looking Backward* and realized in 1893 in the traceries of the interior of the Bradbury building in Los Angeles. It was the sunlit dream that filtered through the sycamores into the patios of the Spanish and Mission revivals. The Mediterranean was in the mind of James D. Phelan, the philanthropist, when he hoped the culture of his San Francisco would blossom like a Renaissance Florence. It would be a city where the arts were fed by the sea air and the sunshine bringing with them the Latin love of life. About the same time in 1903 a writer in *Out West* mused that the minds of future generations would be freshened and inspired as they had been in Rome and Genoa in the Italianesque gardens and landscapes of southern California. The Mediterranean images were on all sides—French vineyards, Greek theatres and temples on Point Loma, camel races in the Date Festival in Indio and in the flavor of whole cities like Santa Barbara and Naples and Venice.

The grandest of the Mediterranean replications, Venice, was the work of Abbott Kinney, a white-bearded, dark-moustached, starry-eyed combination of booster and dreamer. He made his first fortune in cigarettes before he settled in Sierra Madre where he raised citrus. His energy went out to cause after

A Mediterranean fantasy: Venice *c.* 1908

cause—the California Indian, conservation of forests, public libraries, the Australian ballot. All the while he was active in land development, chiefly in Santa Monica and Ocean Park.

He had long imagined that an American Renaissance would take place in southern California, and in 1904 he began work on what he hoped would become the setting, the reproduction of Venice in the New World. With his own travel memories and confidence in his artistic sensibilities, he and his architects duplicated Saint Mark's Square and the Doge's Palace, and dredged sixteen miles of canals plus a grand lagoon flooded with sea water. From Italy he imported two dozen gondoliers with their black and silver gondolas. A 3,600-seat theatre was the hub of the cultural Renaissance. Helen Hunt Jackson, Kinney's colleague in a report on the California Indians, lectured there in a Chautauqua series. Sarah Bernhardt played Camille on its stage. Concerts and cultural exhibits were planned. Potted palms lined the squares and banners hung from the porticoes. At night colored lights reflected in the waters.

In these rare peaceful years before World War I, Venice was a developer's heaven. In the first months, lot sales totaled $386,000. On one holiday in 1910, some thirty-three thousand people arrived from Los Angeles on the big red cars of the Pacific Electric. But by then it was clear that the crowds were not seeking culture. In 1906 Kinney had added a pier with joy rides and hawkers. Cotton candy and salt-water taffy outsold the concerts, jitneys proved more attractive than the gondolas.

Carts of abalone pearl souvenirs replaced the cultural exhibits. By the time of Abbott Kinney's death in 1920 Venice faced serious problems—poor drainage in the canals, erosion of the beach, sewer deficiencies, parking needs for the rising numbers of automobiles. In 1927 most of the canals were filled and paved. Three years later the first oil wells began pumping and discharging a few miles to the south.

In the 1950s and 1960s Venice became a favorite haven for "the broken, the doomed, the drunk and the disillusioned herding together for a little human warmth." It was Henry Miller's Big Sur less the fog and with fewer pines. One of Venice's "holy barbarians," Lawrence Lipton, in the light of a naked electric bulb suspended from the ceiling "like an exposed nerve," looked back on Kinney's vision, "as trite as a penny postal card." Kinney died broken in heart and pocket, Lipton said, "trying to carry his Cook's Tour memories of the historic city on the Adriatic into the twentieth century." Instead of the replication of culture, Venice had become a variegated Bohemia heavy with misfit utopians proclaiming, like Lipton, that "the organic community of men is a community of love," and looking to a world without violence, war, or politics. From their dedicated poverty, they addressed "a raspberry obligato" at the establishment. One English architect who later visited Venice on a warm Sunday morning, watched couples leisurely walking their dogs or casually strolling through the ruins to buy a newspaper. He wondered if Kinney's fantasy of an Italian city had not at long last been realized.[2]

Venice suggested a strain of fantasy in California life, especially in the south. Fantasy is powerful; it can "inspire new civilizations and bring empires to their knees," wrote Harvey Cox.[3] It is to the individual what utopian thinking is to the society, and is often expressed in architecture. In Nathanael West's *Day of the Locust* (1939), Todd Hackett walked down a Hollywood street passing "Mexican ranch houses, Samoan huts, Mediterranean villas, Egyptian and Japanese temples, Swiss chalets, Tudor cottages, and every possible combination of these styles."[4] "Strikingly and lovably ridiculous," was Reyner Banham's phrase for these architectural whimsies, and he concluded, "Los Angeles has seen in this century the greatest concentration of fantasy-production, as an industry and as an institution, in the

"Strikingly and lovably ridiculous": The Tamale (*Courtesy of Special Collections, Research Library, University of California, Los Angeles*)

history of Western man." Motion picture studios and even movie theatres, especially in the 1930s—the Million Dollar, Grauman's Chinese, the Egyptian—spelled romance. Like Potemkin's villages moved around to hoodwink Catherine the Great, miniature golf courses and amusement parks like Disneyland and Magic Mountain have provided instant fantasy. Disneyland in particular since 1955 has thrown its image statewide— a festival of fantastic food and entertainment in the shadow of fabled architecture in which groups happily submit to rigid control amid an illusion of cornucopia and corporate paternalism.[5] Its mythic streets and plazas blissfully free of the strains of capitalism have actually been, like Kinney's Venice or the movie lot, intimately related to promotion and salesmanship, yet they have also stood as backdrops for the imagination of the dreamer and the utopian.

The promoter, however, always has one nonutopian eye on profit. Not so with more radical political and economic reformers like Henry George and Upton Sinclair. Henry George, the red-bearded, bombastic prophet of San Francisco, had as a boy shipped out of his native Philadelphia. In Calcutta he was stirred by sights of poverty, by the enormous gap between maharajas and untouchables. California would indelibly mark him; his great work, *Progress and Poverty* (1879), was, in the words of his biographer, "distinctively and peculiarly Californian." A trip to New York City, though, acted like India to confirm his ideas: as his son later described, "Side by side with the palaces of the princely rich was to be seen a poverty and degradation, a want and shame such as made the young man from the open West sick at heart."[6]

Within a few miles of San Francisco, he observed, there was enough land, if properly used, to give employment to all the poor of the city. But the soil was idle, monopolized by speculators, the worst of which was the railroad. The abolition of private property in land would solve the problem, but George did not require that drastic a remedy. Taxation of the unearned value of land would suffice, if the revenues were returned to the society. It would be "the taking by the community, for the use of the community, of that value which is the creation of the community." The rest of the economy would be freed from the burdens of taxation, and technology would proceed unfettered with its primary business of production for human needs.

The consequent vision in *Progress and Poverty* was indeed inspiring. Trade and wealth would augment on every hand. "The simple but sovereign remedy," the single tax, would raise wages, increase the return on capital, "extirpate pauperism," purify the government that administered this great cooperative society, eliminate crime, and "elevate morals, and taste, and intelligence." George saw "youth no longer stunted and starved; age no longer harried by avarice; the child at play with the tiger; the man with the muck rake drinking in the glory of the stars." "Who should crouch where all were free men; who oppress where all are peers?"[7]

Similar visions occasionally arose from the throes of labor organization in the late nineteenth and early twentieth centuries. John Steinbeck saw that dedication to the future when, in *Dubious Battle* (1936), he described the religious light in a young labor organizer's eyes, "the vision of Heaven." Eugene Debs, one of labor's fiercest spokesmen, once said, "The workers are the saviors of society; the redeemers of the race." If given their way, they will create a world without masters and without slaves, "regenerated and resplendent."[8] He was speaking in 1905, and out of that meeting grew the Industrial Workers of the World, the Wobblies, the most visionary of labor's offspring.

For twenty years afterward, using anarchistic violence when necessary, the IWW fought for one big union and championed certain workers whom the larger movement had passed over— Mexicans, Asians, blacks, lumberjacks, and, most important in California, migrant farm laborers. Strikes by the IWW in Fresno, Wheatland, San Diego, and San Pedro for the right to speak and unionize ended in bloody clashes usually provoked by police and vigilantes. Spurred on by an unusual dream, the Wobblies continued to ride their boxcars to the next confrontation, singing "Hallelujah, I'm a Bum" or "The Big Rock Candy Mountain." They were never as effective as the larger unions, but in their hopes they had no parallel. When their one big union would triumph, poverty would be erased, both material and spiritual. All men would be equal regardless of color. And this small band of militant, chosen people would bring a new society to birth.

One of their strongest leaders, Bill Haywood, later said, "I don't think that I presented any utopian ideas."[9] He meant that he had struggled for practical necessities and believed them attainable. Yet in truth he led a millenarian movement which loved to hear its speakers picture a society without class conflict, without enslavement to the machine. Their songs, with the undying spirit of Joe Hill, were rich with religious implications, like their own ending to "The Battle Hymn of the Republic": "Soon we'll rest beside the fountain and the dreamland will be here, as we go marching on." The present society would give labor nothing but "pie in the sky when you die," but the fists and songs of these men tried to bring about a heaven here on earth.

The Great Depression of the 1930s provoked several movements which did not intend an overthrow but which were revolutionary enough to be considered utopian. Of these the Townsend Movement was the least sweeping in its program.

In 1919, physician Francis Townsend had come from South Dakota to California for his health. Settling in Long Beach, he observed what he called "the boom center of the nation." He liked his new neighbors. If they were "crack pots," that was better than being dullards; at least they were not afraid "to spring a new proposal or suggest a change." As the Great Depression deepened, he was working for the Los Angeles County

Health Department, and he watched the needy suffer. In 1933 he outlined for the Long Beach *Press Telegram* a simple remedy, and his movement had begun. Every person over sixty was to be pensioned monthly with $200 which, because it must be spent within a month, would activate the entire economy. For the necessary petitions and signatures, the response was as booming as land speculation in the 1920s. "Where Christianity ordered its hundreds in its beginning years, our cause orders its millions." One Townsendite near Santa Cruz chanted, "Nothing can stop us, but Almighty God, and God is with us."[10] But the movement died after the New Deal in Washington instituted social security in 1935 and robbed the Townsend Movement of its principal cause.

Meanwhile the depression had unleashed a major reaction to the modern confrontation between frailty and technological efficiency. When Howard Scott, an eastern engineer, asked why there was unemployment and hunger in a country with the capacity of plenty, he pointed his finger at politicians and capitalists who stood in technology's way. The ideal society must be managed by scientists, inventors, and engineers with no thought but the maximizing of production. It would be a world in which kings and parliaments would be supplanted by technical knowledge, rather in the tradition of Saint-Simon, Auguste Comte, and later B. F. Skinner. Nowhere did Scott's vision produce such a mass response as in southern California, where Plenty-for-All clubs mushroomed and "technates" wore steel-gray suits and dresses. In 1933 Scott moved his headquarters to Los Angeles. One teenage enthusiast, Ray Bradbury, felt that Technocracy combined all the hopes and dreams of science fiction. A recent historian has called the movement "the most powerful utopian vision of the late modern world," and it may well have been the most prophetic.[11]

A small group of businessmen and promoters, for whom the parent organization was too steel-gray, broke off from Technocracy in the summer of 1933 to form the Utopian Society. To the intellectual appeal of Technocracy it added the secrecy and comradeship of a fraternal lodge, with rituals, initiations, cycles of advancement, pageants, and social activities in small groups. It continued to champion a triumphant technology without private ownership and profit, a world which would require no one to work more than three hours a day. Education would last until the age of twenty-five and pensions would begin at forty-five. Using chain letters, they could readily fill the huge Shrine Auditorium or the Hollywood Bowl for their events. Carey McWilliams, a young reporter covering the society, estimated its numbers at half a million in the Los Angeles area alone. Every night they held at least 250 meetings in the region.

It was a heady time for utopia, and 1934 saw a socialist vision reach deep into the heart of traditional California politics. Upton Sinclair's program to "End Poverty in California" was too radical for Francis Townsend. Sinclair was a much older Californian than Townsend, having lived in the state for some twenty-five years. In New York, he had been converted to socialism and in 1905 organized a club that sponsored lectures like Jack London. The following year Sinclair published his muckraking novel *The Jungle* (1906), exposing corporate corruption and unsanitary conditions in the meatpacking industry. It was a powerful but humane book, like Sinclair's socialism, rooted in Christianity and democracy with little of the brusque violence of Jack London.

Sinclair first came to California for a visit at the urging of two of his socialist friends, Gaylord Wilshire and the poet George Sterling. Sinclair had been involved with the disappointing end of a utopian colony called Helicon Hall in New Jersey (1906–1907). For personal reasons, too, he was on the verge of a nervous breakdown, so he went to California to find his health again. He first joined Wilshire, who was then trying to run a mining camp on socialist principles. Before becoming a socialist Wilshire had won and lost a fortune in real estate in west Los Angeles, where the main boulevard still bears his name. Sinclair stayed a while with Wilshire, then went over to Carmel where he visited Sterling and began experimenting with a raw food diet.

In 1915 Sinclair returned again from the East to California, this time to stay for the rest of his life. In the 1920s he entered politics with unsuccessful runs as a socialist for Congress, the Senate, and governor of the state. Then came the depression, which hit California hard, as it did Sinclair's sensibilities. One and a quarter million people were on relief. In such circumstances Governor James Rolph's veto of an income tax and the imposition of a sales tax on food seemed heartless. Long before, in 1912, Sinclair had written a utopian treatise called *The Industrial Republic* in which he had imagined William Randolph Hearst elected president, ending a financial panic, and moving America peacefully into socialism. Now Sinclair hoped to accomplish something similar by running for state office. In his pamphlet "I, Governor of California," he outlined his EPIC plan.

Sinclair proposed to remove the unemployed to agricultural and industrial colonies, not unlike the nineteenth-century plans of Robert Owen or Charles Fourier. The workers could wrest some of the means of production from the business autocracy. "We must summon the courage to take the wild beast of greed by the beard." The colonies would have good housing, cooperative kitchens, and plenty of opportunity for physical and intellectual development through libraries, cinemas, and lectures. Women could work because of child-care centers, and there would be maternal as well as old-age pensions. Through a scrip system, the extra production would go to the needy and the hungry. Once in operation the plan would pay its own way since it was production solely for use, not for profit. Sinclair imagined his address to the first colonists: "You have only common sense, human brotherhood, and the Christian religion on your side."[12] These were the pillars of his utopia, placed beneath an ideal community which had been erected on the ravages of depression.

Yet this mild socialism was realistic enough that the Democratic Party nominated Sinclair as its candidate for governor. He was not supported by the national party, and conservatives in the state, especially in the motion picture industry, fought him viciously. The Republican incumbent, Frank Merriam, won by a margin of twenty-three percent. After his defeat, Sinclair organized another EPIC movement to "End Poverty in Civilization." With it he tried in 1936 to win the California delegation to the Democratic national convention. He was rejected and as a result withdrew from politics. Nevertheless, with men like Sheridan Downey and Culbert Olson having filtered through the EPIC program, California's Democratic Party, for at least a generation, would be tinged with unusual idealism. Still, until Sinclair died in 1968, he remained the symbol of democratic socialism in the tradition of Henry George; he was a populist dreamer who had come closer than any other visionary to capturing the state for utopia.

# Utopia
# as Millennium

I N 1888 Mary Stewart Daggett, a young woman of twenty-nine, came from Ohio to settle in Pasadena. In the shadow of "the prophetic mountains" she felt her analytic tendencies weaken, her beliefs grow more unorthodox, and her "pagan intuitions" expand. Seven years after her arrival, she wrote "I am told that the millennium has already begun in Pasadena, and that even now there are more sanctified cranks to the acre than in any other town in America."[1] Mary Daggett was experiencing and expressing what would become a ritual cliché about California. As Curt Gentry put it with no shred of proof, California's "mild climate spawned more bizarre religious and utopian schemes than the rest of the states put together."[2]

Religion by its very nature can be a springboard of utopianism, because it provides an ideal, a motivation, and hopes for regeneration with new beginnings. But in California in the decades after the Gold Rush, traditional Protestant denominations caught the expansive frontier optimism and raised to an extraordinary pitch their missionary expectations. Clergymen like Joseph Benton in Sacramento or Charles Wadsworth and Samuel Willey in San Francisco talked of a glorious future, of a true city on a hill. Timothy Hunt saw California as the new Pilgrim dream. They were like young Thomas Starr King, a crusader of hope during the four short years before he died, having answered his call to California to lay new moral foundations where civilization was weaving "the best threads of the American character."[3] These sanguine expectations, as Kevin Starr said, were often lost in the gradual acceptance of a pluralistic society, and the grandeur of the purpose caused the disappointments to be felt all the more acutely.

The Mormons in San Bernardino were a model of the rise and fall of hopes. They confidently built their stockade outpost in 1851 to help other Saints reach their religious and temporal home by the Great Salt Lake. In so doing they created a cooperative theocracy of church and school and farm, rather like the Pilgrim dream of Timothy Hunt. For a time they achieved "peace without and good order within."[4] By 1857 the rising non-Mormon population, internal conflict, and Brigham Young's need for consolidation in Utah, all brought to an end the experiment below the Cajon Pass, and most of the Saints returned to their Zion at Salt Lake.

Disappointments, the acceptance of pluralism, the growth of Mary Daggett's "pagan intuitions," and the rootlessness of society worked toward an explosion of new religious visions and a willingness to follow charismatic voices. In the twentieth century at least, a fringe of the population capitalized on an increasing tendency toward self-indulgence which caused new cults to thrive. The millennium was at hand, whether in Mary Daggett's Pasadena, Katherine Tingley's Point Loma, or Swami Yogananda's Encinitas. It was reflected in the eyes of every rising guru and evangelist.

An early manifestation of such charismatic utopianism was the Fountain Grove colony of Thomas Lake Harris, set up two miles north of Santa Rosa in 1875. Harris was a western version of John Humphrey Noyes with extra doses of spiritualism and mysticism. In the psychic ideas of Emanuel Swedenborg, the eighteenth-century Swedish theologian, he had found "the noblest system to reform mankind." Through a Divine Respiration man could commune directly with God. Harris preached of "electrovital forces," a bisexual deity, and celibacy for his followers. He sought a "new harmonic civilization," a theosocialism based on small cooperative units without private property or disease.[5] Its creative leader would be Harris, "the pivotal man." He was well endowed for the role with patriarchal beard, resonant voice, and searching eyes.

His community, the Brotherhood of the New Life, looked "for richer revelations to come." Its seventeen hundred acres were mostly planted in grapes—cabernet, pinot noir, zinfandel—and by 1886 seventy thousand gallons of wine were being pressed annually. The community believed its vintages to be infused with its own fraternal love, a "divine and celestial energy." Fountain Grove included six main buildings, dominated by Aestivossa, a Victorian mansion with high ceilings, paneled walls, thick carpets, a library, and stained-glass windows with angels and knights. There was much music and poetry at the communal dining, and at times the ladies' dance group performed quadrilles "until the house quivered."

In the early 1890s, newspapers of Santa Rosa and San Francisco charged Harris with immorality, sexual license, and enslavement of members. In 1892, Harris decided it best for the colony that he leave. Without him the membership slowly drifted apart, and Fountain Grove's wines remained the chief memory of its years as a mystical Eden.

Aimée Semple McPherson set a similar charismatic tone for Los Angeles. From 1918 till her death in 1944 her golden hair, white robes, and the modulations of her magnificent voice drew crowds to her Four Square Gospel Church, where she heralded the imminent coming of the kingdom. Live, she said, as if Christ will arrive any moment and then mankind would glory in perfection. A separated people were readying themselves to walk in the immaculate society.

The same year that Sister Aimée opened her temple in Los Angeles, Father William E. Riker of San Francisco began to buy acreage between San Jose and Santa Cruz. It would become his Holy City, headquarters of "the world's most perfect government." Riker, a native Californian who proudly disavowed book learning, devised a Perfect Christian Divine Way based on spiritualistic messages through his nerves. His followers, no more than thirty-five at any one time, were mostly European immigrants. In their Zion among the redwoods they raised cabins, a gas station, a restaurant, barber and print shops. Huge primitive signboards in the shape of Santa Claus carried messages like "If

Headquarters of the "world's most perfect government": Holy City, 1951

you are contemplating marriage, suicide, or crime, see us first," or "Dispel the idea that you are different from God or the other fellow, when sifted down." Riker loved metaphors: mankind was divided like a human body, a head being the Jews; the trunk, the Gentiles; the arms, Orientals; the legs, Negroes. The white race was intended to direct all the others. Riker, a member of the Ku Klux Klan after 1935, continued to preach that desegregation was race murder, releasing disease and other dreadful evils. After 1952 the membership dwindled to twelve. One member of sixty-eight years proclaimed the faith: "Holy City belongs to mankind, and mankind never dies."

We are still to close to the charismatic utopians of our own day to assess their story adequately, but clearly California continues to produce or encourage them. In 1968, David Brandt Berg opened a coffee house, Teens for Christ, in Huntington Beach. By 1971 four thousand of his followers, the Children of God, were pledged to fight against "Godless schools, Christless churches, and heartless Mammon." Berg assumed the role of a recluse, communicating through letters, and so coordinating what remains a widely dispersed, international movement.

In 1965 Jim Jones began preaching socialism and racial brotherhood in northern California. His People's Temple worked hard for the just society, helping the poor, the drug addicts, and the elderly. Though the appeal to the downtrodden and minority was strong, the means to change were through an unquestioning obedience to the messianic nature of Jim Jones, ultimately demonstrated by the mass suicide of more than 900 members with their leader in Guyana.

Charles Manson in the 1960s carried some of Riker's racism and a good deal of his magnetic appeal. One of his followers, Leslie Van Houten, who had previously taken up reincarnation and karma with the Self-Realization Fellowship, believed that the Manson family was "one with earth and each other." But such a state was accomplished through a loss of personal identity and the substituted sway of what another follower called "the beautiful man." Manson could eventually lead his people without thinking to the multiple stabbing of seven defenseless persons. While picturing this violence as a reflection of American society, Manson at the time of his sentencing calmly said, "In my mind's eye my thoughts light fires in your cities."[6] To the end his was the charisma of brooding eyes lighted with apocalyptic fires.

Charisma provides at best only a partial insight into religious utopianism. Sometimes the leaders, though charismatic, were parts of larger movements attracted to California as another Eden. Theosophy, for example, came in 1897 to Point Loma north of San Diego bay. Dedicating the Universal Brotherhood and Theosophical Society, Katherine Tingley in purple robes laid the cornerstone, "a perfect square," she said, "a fitting emblem of the perfect work that will be done in the temple for the benefit of humanity and glory of the ancient sages."

Katherine Tingley, a vigorous woman with large frame, dark hair, and gray restless eyes, had converted to Theosophy in New York City in 1893. That was where Helena Blavatsky, the Russian occultist, had founded the society eighteen years earlier. The movement had spread across the continent, numbering a hundred lodges by the 1890s, the largest proportion of which was in California.

For some years after Helena Blavatsky's death, leadership of the society was segmented. By 1896 among the potential heirs were two remarkable women. One was Annie Besant, former atheist and Fabian Socialist, now turned Theosophist, who

Birthplace of a higher humanity: Theosophical Institute of Point Loma, *c.* 1920 (*Courtesy of History Division, Los Angeles County Museum of Natural History*)

helped set up a headquarters in India and became the chief voice from the Far East. The other was Katherine Tingley, whose thinking tended to deemphasize mysticism and the occult in favor of Theosophical doctrines on the brotherhood of man. She represented a strain that in the 1890s was intimate with Edward Bellamy's Nationalist Clubs, especially in California. For her the study of Eastern religions was an exploration of the common denominator in human experience. Psychic phenomena were undeniable, but Tingley cautioned her followers in the present stage of evolution to avoid their dangers.

From about 1900 until her death in 1929 Katherine Tingley devoted her energy to the community on Point Loma. At its height about 1907 she ruled a domain of 330 acres and a population of five hundred people. Two of the main buildings were surmounted by aquamarine and amethyst glass domes illuminated from within at night. There were groups of bungalows and tents, a Greek theater, avenues winding through luxuriant gardens, orchards, and forests of eucalyptus, all on previously barren ground.

Katherine Tingley looked upon Point Loma as the concrete

expression of the ideals of Theosophy, "a practical illlustration of the possibility of developing a higher type of humanity."[7] Harrison Gray Otis of the *Los Angeles Times,* self-appointed guardian of the region against cultism, saw it differently. He described Point Loma as "the spookery," surrounded by armed men under the "strong hypnotic power" of the Purple Mother. Tingley's consequent libel suit against Otis awarded her $7,500 in damages.

Life for the ascending human race was disciplined and orderly. There was even a military tone to the men's loose uniforms and the boys' morning drills. Children were raised away from their parents but under careful surveillance. Responsibilities to the group were underscored along with a perfect balance of all the faculties—mental, physical, and spiritual. Success would lead to higher levels of reincarnation. Music and drama were central. The Raja Yoga International Orchestra played proud performances, and the Greek Theater, looking out to the open sea, amplified the words of Aeschylus and Shakespeare. Every play was a gigantic community effort down to the smallest child pasting paper flowers. But the community received the praise, since individuals, even the leading actors, remained anonymous.

"There is a top rung to every ladder," Katherine Tingley once wrote. As leader for life with the power to choose her successor, she held her position with honor and dignity. Her accidental death at the age of seventy-nine was a blow, coupled as it was with the great crash of 1929. In the drastic retrenchments the glory faded. In the 1940s, financial stability was restored. The society moved to Covina and later to Pasadena. It never tried, however, to recreate that realm of cultured cooperation through which Katherine Tingley had woven her dreams.

In 1903 a physician, William E. Dower, also brought a group of Theosophists from Syracuse, New York, to the sand dunes south of Pismo Beach, naming the settlement Halcyon. Dower spoke of love and harmony conquering all abnormality and disease and reforming mankind. The work at Halcyon revolved around a three-stored sanatorium, an ingenious three-sided and colonnaded Temple of the People, and a cooperative living association, Temple Home. Among the latter were mild socialists who found Eugene Debs and Upton Sinclair moving in the same direction as Theosophy. The membership, which grew to fifty within a few years, lived on half-acre plots and raised vegetables, sugar beets, and flower seeds. Their enjoyment of swimming and picnicking together was to them a sign of the new dispensation, the dawn light of the Age of Aquarius, a time of brotherhood and reunification. By 1912 financial stringencies and personal conflicts struck down the economically cooperative aspects of Temple Home, but the Temple of the People carried on. In the 1970s its resident members numbered about twenty-five, kept vigorous by a wave of young converts seeking mysticism, simplicity, and rural life.[8]

Ojai, too, has been a major Theosophical center, conceived as the germinal environment for a renewed human race. In 1924 a Theosophist, Albert P. Warrington, moved his Krotona colony there from the Hollywood hills. Warrington owed allegiance to the Far Eastern branch, associated with Annie Besant, and hence communicated little with Point Loma or Halcyon. He had earlier told young Jiddu Krishnamurti about Ojai, and Krishnamurti had visited and loved it. As a boy in India about 1910, Krishnamurti had been identified by Besant as a messianic vehicle of the ascended masters. In 1926 he, in turn, introduced her to Ojai. She was entranced and bought 450 acres. Besant felt Ojai to be a place of special magnetism and foresaw it as a hub of world religions. Krishnamurti made it his home and headquarters. Though in time he renounced his messianic nature, he could still claim, lecturing to his followers under the oak trees, that Ojai had been for him as for Annie Besant a valley of unusual mystical spirituality.

Theosophy is a reminder of how often Eastern or neo-Oriental religions have found in California a place of singular meaning. In 1899, two years after Katherine Tingley dedicated Point Loma, Swami Vivekananda introduced Vedanta to California. The California Vedantists expanded with later adherents like Gerald Heard, Aldous Huxley, and Christopher Isherwood until in the 1950s they included three active churches, two monasteries, a convent, and a third of the American membership. Likewise, Swami Paramahansa Yogananda instituted his international headquarters of the Self-Realization Fellowship in Los Angeles in 1925. He claimed twenty-five thousand followers before his death in 1952. By then the Fellowship's centers on Mount Washington, in Hollywood, and overlooking the sea

A meeting of East and West: the Self-Realization Fellowship at Encinitas
(*Courtesy of San Diego Historical Society*)

at Encinitas symbolized through architecture, dietary habits, and meditative practices another meeting of East and West.[9]

Most of the other Oriental sects in California have been smaller or more ephemeral. But they have been numerous. Long before the 1960s, telephone directories and religion pages of the larger newspapers were studded with names like Krishna, Yogi Hari Rama, Yogessar, the Aum Temple, or the Messianic World Message of A. K. Mozumdar. The Mazdaznan sect in the 1950s sought health and higher consciousness through a union of Zarathustra and Jesus. The Rosicrucians in their unrelated establishments at San Jose and Oceanside looked for upward reincarnation through astrology and the lore of ancient Egypt. Some, like the Institute of Mental Physics, clothed Oriental techniques with scientific terminology. But most worked through ascended masters and added the flavor of Tibetan mysteries to their pursuit of personal psychic energy. So it was with the I Am cult of the 1930s, product of peculiar spiritual forces descending upon a mining engineer, Guy Ballard, on the slopes of Mt. Shasta.

The extensive "turning East" of the 1970s, as Harvey Cox has said, came to a generation disillusioned by philosophies like the death of God and disappointed in the hopes of the late 1960s.[10] Neo-Orientalism has touched several million Americans, a major proportion of whom have been Calfornians. In their attraction to the strange and remote, these tend to be withdrawing from social concern, introspectively searching for personal spiritual experience. True, the social consequences of the higher consciousness are never far removed. Swami Kriyananda, disciple of Yogananda and founder of the Ananda colony near Nevada City, actively leads communitarian movements as we will see. But most of the Orientalists are only indirectly interested in social or utopian ventures.

If the Eastern groups have been withdrawn in their utopianism, the Western have probably taken the reverse path. In the early 1890s, while Mary Daggett was finding the millennium in Pasadena, Edward Biron Payne, the Unitarian minister of Berkeley, was rallying such an outward-looking social-gospel movement called Altruria. Its most publicized effort was a colony in Sonoma Valley, but it also produced five clubs in the areas of San Francisco and Los Angeles. The name derived from a current utopian novel by William Dean Howells, *A Traveler from Altruria* (1893). In it a Mr. Homos from a distant ideal society visited America, asked embarrassing questions, and described the harmonious order of his own country. This Altruria was a land of communal ownership and short working hours where modern machinery had been outlawed. The picture fitted with Payne's other Christian socialist ideas, taken from works of clerics like George D. Herron. With them he looked forward to nonviolent change accomplished through worker-controlled, cooperative units.

Payne, as a young Congregationalist minister fresh from Oberlin College, had been called to California in 1875, like Thomas Starr King before him, to lay moral foundations. Reading journals like *The Dawn,* he had been radicalized, and he moved into Unitarianism. His church was, as one member said, "flooded by the benediction of his spirit."[11]

In 1894 eighteen adults and eight children from among Payne's congregation joyfully set up Altruria on 185 acres just north of Fountain Grove, which Thomas Lake Harris had left only two years before. The nation was in the midst of a major

depression, yet the colonists' extravagant plans for the cooperative spiritual life spilled over into economic fantasies. They
imagined a future based on presumed coal and aluminum de-
posits, hydroelectric power, a manmade lake, and on its shores a
grand hotel brimming with tourists. Jack London's Elam Harnish could not have dreamed more ebulliently. The hotel was
actually begun, and by the spring of 1895 its kitchen and dining
room were functioning. The remaining two stories, however,
were never finished, and their jutting beams hinted at the heavy
drain in energy and capital. Not that it worried Altrurians much,
for the days were filled with recitals, holiday merriment, inspiring sermons under the trees, and rewarding cooperative labor.
Those who saw more deeply, though, noted impending financial
chaos. In the second year of the colony's life, trouble became
evident. The local clubs tried to help; they sent a cow, a chess
set, and small donations. Nevertheless, in 1895 the colony broke
up into smaller parts, and these, along with the clubs, in time
became local cooperatives for food buying, baking, and laundry-
ing. Actually they were not far from their aim of small cooperative units based on spiritual unity, and the new approach was
probably more realistic than the colony in a time of depressed
economic conditions. The rearrangement hardly justified Ambrose Bierce's derision of the Altrurians as "amiable asses." The
consumer cooperative movement, after all, never died, and
even the Altrurian colonists always recalled their experience in
the Sonoma Valley as a warm and happy year in their lives.

Similarly outward-looking was Father Finis Yoakum's Pisgah.
Before World War I, Yoakum applied his faith and his social
gospel to the skid rows of Los Angeles with settlement houses
for the unemployed, delinquent, and sick. In 1914 he conceived
a more elaborate branch, Pisgah Grande, removed from the city
in the Santa Susana Mountains beyond the San Fernando Valley.
On over three thousand wooded acres he created his city of
God, including a central house, a communal dining hall, smaller
dwellings, a school, post office, and a watch tower for eternal
prayer and vigil. Seventy-five residents from the Los Angeles
mission helped usher in the kingdom that remained active until
after Yoakum's death in 1920.[12]

Mankind United was also a social-gospel cult fostered, like
Upton Sinclair's EPIC, by the Great Depression. Between 1934

and 1941 it recruited fourteen thousand members, mostly elderly or unemployed. On joining, they surrendered their remaining worldly possessions to the group. Its revelations included magical rays and trances from which a social message was drawn. On achieving the critical number of two hundred million, members of Mankind United would have to work for only four hours a day, four days a week, eight months a year. Pensions would begin at sixty, and each family would live in a $25,000 house, amazingly well equipped. The cult was a curious combination of economic need, ethereal visions, and pathetic hopes for a better world.

The charismatic and millenarian religions of California, whether turning East or West, looking inward or outward, have strongly mirrored utopianism. They have prophesied perfection, either in the human race or in the society they have foreseen. For them, California regions like Ojai or Mt. Shasta have often been mystical locales for the regeneration of mankind. As with Bret Harte or Henry Miller, they have thus reveled in a sense of peculiar place. The clear and present prospect of political revolution was for them weak or missing, but in its stead were the ethics of optimism and the recurring expectations of paradise.

# The Experimental Commitment

E VERY EXPERIMENTAL colonist with whom Aldous Huxley ever talked held, he said, "a sustaining conviction that one had broken out of an age-old prison and was marching, shoulder to shoulder with loyal comrades, towards a promised land."[1] How could it be otherwise for those whose aching for the ideal society had compelled them to withdraw from a familiar world to refashion their lives? Their commitment to change motivated at least a temporary behavioral modification, and the collective model would provide a beacon for others. Skeptics might describe that light as no more than a sputtering candle, but in fact most experiments were in fundamental traditions of reform, traditions that avoided the violence of political revolution in favor of precept and emulation.

In 1883 in the foothills of Sonoma County a band of French people calling themselves Icaria Speranza signed articles of agreement. "Community based on solidarity," they affirmed, "is realizable and possible."[2] Some fifty-five of them were in the process of migrating from their parent commune in Iowa to farm land near Cloverdale. They were the younger and more radical of the Icarians, heirs to a utopian and revolutionary line that ran back to a French novelist, Étienne Cabet. His *Voyage en*

*Icarie* in 1840 had inspired five hundred Frenchmen to leave home and demonstrate a better way in America. After trials in Texas and Illinois, they ended in Iowa where their island of Gallic socialism persisted for thirty years. In 1881 the Dehay and Leroux families moved to California and gathered the Bée and Provost families to form Icaria Speranza. Émile Bée, a radical from San Francisco, had fought like many other Icarians on the barricades at the Paris Commune of 1871. He and Armand Dehay, who had given up his trade of barber in France to become a farmer in Icaria, now began to write their comrades in Iowa. They described the sheltered valleys with heady air like fine wine, and they pressed flowers into the paper to show how California blossomed while Iowa shivered. In time their friends joined them to draft their new agreement in California.

The arrangement set up common ownership of the 850 acres and all means of production, but half of each annual surplus was to be divided among the members. They produced a fine zinfandel wine, also wheat, peaches, and prunes. Clothes and furniture and smaller items were privately owned, but the clothes were designed and sewn communally. Members dined together in a large central house, though marriage and the family were considered basic to their life. Believing "the true practice of fraternity" to be their highest form of worship, they looked on competition as the great ethical evil, the essential illness of mankind.

Icaria Speranza, having manifested its ideals for five years, was dissolved in 1887. It had always demanded that recruits speak French; thus its membership pool was highly restricted. But more important, some of its members worried that their experiment had too little to offer the poor and the suffering of the world. These drifted off to apply their radicalism to more urgent social situations. Watching the end, Armand Dehay wrote, "My heart is broken that our commune is crushed," but over forty years later his wife maintained, "The principle stays, and in time will be perfected. That is my belief."

The Icarians probably knew some of the sixty-eight men who met in San Francisco on the night of November 9, 1884. The chairman of that meeting was Burnette G. Haskell, a twenty-seven-year-old lawyer, organizer of the city's International Working Men's Association. His was the rhetoric of the Marx-

"The true practice of fraternity": Icaria Speranza, *c.* 1887

ian First International—"The proletarians have nothing to lose but their chains. They have a world to win." But along with his socialism, Haskell may have been California's most genuine native utopian.

Born in Sierra County, Haskell came to San Francisco to study law and later to edit a newspaper, *Truth*. On editorial missions he became interested in the trade union movement and the cause of the working man. His life would thereafter be a series of espousals, like Edward Bellamy's Nationalism, a ritualistic order called the Invisible Republic, and Populism—all consistent in faith for the perfection of mankind.

The men that Haskell assembled that November night were fired with plans for a socialist colony. Most of them had read Laurence Gronlund's *Cooperative Commonwealth* (1884), recently published as the first treatise on Marxism by "a writer possessing the American bias for the practical." In it Gronlund had sketched the framework of an ideal community. The immediate worry of the San Francisco gathering, however, was not the plan of a colony but its location and the related economic base. That issue was surmounted shortly afterward when Haskell learned of government timberlands opening for entry along the Kaweah River in eastern Tulare County.

So in the fall of 1885, fifty-three men of Kaweah filed on

government land and then tramped with surveyors over their claims. The parcels stretched from the gentle foothills to the Giant Redwood Forest of the future Sequoia National Park. The timber on the higher elevations had been declared commercially inaccessible but the colony scorned capitalistic conclusions. It seriously planned a road up the mountain with railroad and canal to tidewater, and its own ships carrying lumber, olive oil, honey, fruit, and wine into world commerce.

The number of residents in the colony averaged from fifty to seventy-five during most of its days, but as many as four hundred people lived there at one time or another. William Carey Jones of the University of California's law school visited Kaweah and was impressed with its quality—"intelligent, thoughtful, earnest, readers of books and journals, alive to the great economic and social names of the day." Behind the resident members stood a network of local clubs from Los Angeles to New York. Laurence Gronlund, for example, joined the movement in Boston.

Philip Winser heard of Kaweah on his family farm in Kent, England. With a dissenting Unitarian background, he had been pondering the "anomalies of society," had read Edward Bellamy and, writing to Boston for further literature, had received a pamphlet on the California colony. He was so inspired that he sold his farm, fitted out a tool box, folded under his arm the hammock he had slept in since a boy, and sailed from Liverpool. In Boston he attended a Nationalist Club where he met Edward Bellamy. The great man shook his head over Kaweah; no such experiment, Bellamy thought, could succeed on less than a national scale. Undaunted, Winser crossed the continent and arrived in Kaweah on a cold February day, eager to prove that cooperation could save mankind. He found others who had come less far but whose illusions were equally grand. Here man shall have "such freedom for growth and development that he, like some golden pinnacle of a perfect palace, shall tower far above the foundation walls."

There was little luxury at Kaweah. Tents were a principal shelter until 1889. Lumber then began to come down from the mill and cabins rose around a community center for dining and assemblies. A barn, print shop, blacksmith's shop, and a community store were nearby. Daily life was hard but enjoyable.

"Dress-reform cranks, and phonetic spelling fanatics, word purists and vegetarians": Camp Advance, Kaweah, *c.* 1886


The Kaweah orchestra played concerts on summer evenings. Adult classes read literature and science and a Home Circle discussed family problems. A Bellamy Nationalist Club met every Wednesday night. Kaweahans danced, swam in the river, picnicked, and camped in the Giant Forest. They named the largest redwoods for socialist heroes. The tree they called the Karl Marx is now more widely known as the General Sherman.

Building of the colony road up the mountain into the timber began within a year of settlement. For four years the road painstakingly took shape, consuming energies that probably should have gone to crops and orchards. Some of the route was picked and shoveled by hand across precipitous granite ledges. It wound for eighteen miles to an altitude of eight thousand feet, reaching the pines in June 1890. Long after the area became Sequoia National Park, this road was the only access to the Giant Forest.

Once a month the colony ceased its labor for a general meeting. The debates were vehement and on a few occasions lasted for several days. Blacksmith Dudley refused to quit work and rang his anvil louder in protest over the endless argumentation. They discussed the powers of the board of trustees. A system of

time checks in which all labor was equally valued at thirty cents
an hour was good for endless review, as was the membership fee
of $500, most of which was payable in goods or labor. There
were bitter disputes over whether the colony should become a
joint-stock company or whether a complete list of nonresident
members should be printed. These latter issues actually caused
blocks of members to secede. Haskell blamed the disruptions
on the variegated idealism: "There were dress-reform cranks,
and phonetic spelling fanatics, word purists and vegetarians. It
was a mad, mad world." He remembered seeing a woman chop-
ping wood in plain sight of thirteen idle men who for six hours
had argued over a point of order. "Little pin pricks," he said,
"killed the noble purpose and enthusiasm of the enterprise and
slowly drained its life away."

Haskell himself as a leader proved to be argumentative and
undependable. His personality abraded others, often into open
rupture. Yet what probably hurt Kaweah most were not internal
maladies but external hostilities. Eventually the federal government, the courts, the press, and possibly the timber and railroad
interests engaged in attacks or animosities. The General Land
Office in Washington suspended Kaweah's land claims shortly
after they were made, and year after year refused to dispose of
the case one way or another.

The land agents were initially suspicious that the colony was a
front for the Southern Pacific Railroad, but these socialists considered the rumor too ridiculous to take seriously. After four
years of procrastination, the Land Office was relieved of the
issue in 1890 when Congress created Sequoia National Park.
The legislation affected most of the colony's land. Kaweah's
only recourse, which never succeeded, was to seek reimburse-
ment for both the lands and improvements. Legally the government was not bound to pay because the colonists never held full
title. But since Kaweah had acted in good faith the legal position
was hardly just.

The press from Visalia to San Francisco delighted in derision
and innuendo—"deluded beings," "miserable people," "villain-
ous gang," "tools of the lumber barons," "infamous bunco
game," "this mountain trap." As for the courts, in 1891 the
colony was charged with cutting five pine trees on public lands.
In truth during the first days after the road had reached timber,

the boundary had been overstepped, but the mistake was quickly corrected. The district court in Los Angeles nevertheless found the trustees guilty and fined them from $100 to $300 each. In 1892 the colony again had to defend itself, this time on charges of using the mails to defraud. In this case the judge instructed the jury to acquit on grounds of insufficient evidence.

But by then Kaweah was already in disarray. A reduced number of residents lived on the few acres left after the creation of the national park. They wrangled over disposition of the remaining assets. One member shot himself. Haskell, waiting for the trial of 1891 to begin, once thought he had discovered gold. He promised his diary to use the possible fortune "to practically make human beings better." Later he reviewed his dismembered Kaweah, "one of the hopes of my life." "And is there remedy, then," he asked, "for the evils that oppress the poor? And is there no surety that the day is coming when justice and right shall reign on earth? I do not know; but I believe, and I hope, and I trust."

Kaweah's memory was bright for Irastus Kelsey in 1893 when he organized the Brotherhood of Winters Island. An Ohioan, educated at the University of Michigan, Kelsey had become a farmer in California, owning land in the rich delta behind San Francisco Bay. He was always politically oriented, a leader in the farmers' alliance, Bellamy's Nationalism, and the Populist party. Now he proposed to use his land, Winters Island, as the base for a colony on the Kaweah model. He thought of asking Haskell to help, but instead found Kate Lockwood Nevins, a vigorous activist, and together they enrolled a hundred members by July 1893. Probably no more than twenty or thirty of them were residents at any one time. The Islanders owned the land, buildings, and tools in common, worked cooperatively, and divided the profits equally. They built levees around most of the 638 acres, planted orchards and about seventy acres each in hay and vegetables. Onions were their most successful crop.

Unfortunately the depression following 1893, as with their fellow cooperators at Altruria, hit the colonists hard. By 1898 the long battle against sagging prices finally sapped the last enthusiasm. Only a few stragglers were left, the last being Kate Nevins, who remained alone on the colony lands until she died.

In the political ferment of the 1890s in San Francisco a young man was taking steps which would ultimately place him at the head of the most extensive utopian experiment California has known. Job Harriman in 1886 had come to California as a footloose lawyer, and his leanings toward Christian Socialism had started him on a familiar path—Bellamy's Nationalism, Altrurian clubs, locals of the Socialist Labor Party. He was slender, delicately featured, with a mop of dark hair, a willingness to elevate a cause over his own well-being, and an ability to call forth magnums of loyalty. In the late 1890s he was pushed forward into politics, nominated for governor of California on the Socialist ticket and in 1900 for vice-president of the United States with Eugene Debs.

After he removed his law practice to Los Angeles, the Socialist Party there nominated him for mayor. That was in 1910, a critical year for the working class in southern California. The bombing of the *Los Angeles Times* that year left twenty dead, and blame fell upon the labor unions. In the defense of the McNamara brothers, two of the indicted laborers, Harriman was one of the chief counselors. When on December 1, 1911, the McNamaras changed their plea to guilty, it was only five days before the municipal elections, and the gutters of Los Angeles were littered with discarded Harriman buttons. He came surprisngly close to victory, but he did lose, and it was his last political venture. Henceforth an economic approach would be his avenue to the better world, and in particular a concrete example of the cooperative life.

Searching for an experimental site, he discovered a nearly defunct company with a large tract of land in the Antelope Valley, part of the Mojave Desert east of Los Angeles. He interested a few socialist families, and raised enough money for a down payment. By 1914 resident members were enthusiastically settling the new colony. Their name was taken from a nearby creek, Llano Del Rio, and the association with water was an augury which time would twist into trouble.

The initial families within a few years had expanded to nine hundred members. As at Kaweah, tents and temporary structures were necessary during most of the colony's life. The exception was a community hotel with walls of native boulders furnishing a few rooms, a dining and assembly hall, and a fireplace where blazing juniper fires gave warmth on winter nights.

Harriman hired feminist architect Alice Constance Austin, whose philosophy of communal planning called for private gardens balanced with neighborhood parks; common utilities, heating, food preparation, and laundry; and small private kitchens intended to make women's housework minimal.[3] Unfortunately, like Burnham's plans for San Francisco, time and resources never allowed their realization.

"This colony has progressed," Harriman wrote, "from a utopian chimerical idea to a concrete practicality, from a dozen dreamers to a thousand determined doers."[4] On entrance each new member was required to buy two thousand dollars' worth of stock, but up to three quarters of this could be paid off over a six-year period with labor at the colony. In return came the assurance of employment at four dollars a day with food, clothing, and shelter at cost. Cooperative muscle cleared the land of creosote and burro bush, removed hundreds of wagon loads of rocks, and ran ditches of creek water to the fields. Perhaps the fact that forty percent of the residents were former farmers accounted for the impressive agricultural results—four hundred acres of alfalfa, two hundred acres in cotton, and one hundred acres of orchard, mostly pears. For a time the colony grew a major proportion of its own food, but exporting surplus was always a problem with only two trucks for the entire operation and the railroad connection at Palmdale twenty miles away.

Each two weeks the residents met in general assembly and debated at length everything from socialist theory to the value of planting turnips. Like a national congress in opposition to the president, the assembly never seemed to agree with the seven-member board of directors. One colonist thought of the assembly as "democracy rampant, belligerent, unrestricted, a monster which threatened to destroy the colony." Behind this political machinery, however, a superintendent and small board of managers ran the day-to-day affairs with quiet efficiency. Perhaps it was understandable that the open debates were so raucous because of the many ex-Wobblies, socialists, and former experimenters, all so desperately hoping that the dream should work this time. In any case disgruntled factions became part of the scene at Llano. One in 1915 met among the creosote bushes, carried sprigs for identification as it marched into the general meeting, and gave rise to the epithet "brush gang" for all future malcontents. In the same way, colonists coined a word for shirking work, "gibbonitis," from comrade Gibbons who was mysteriously afflicted with aches and pains whenever labor beckoned.

Education was central to Llano. For the 125 children in 1917 the system included California's first and largest Montessori kindergarten. The elementary grades conformed to the public schools and received tax funds. But the colony added its own industrial school in which older students were required to learn a trade. For adults there were classes for everyone from mandolin players to outdoorsmen, all supplemented by a library of several thousand volumes. Baseball games livened Saturday afternoons; dances, Wednesday and Saturday nights. Sunday evenings saw orchestra performances, plays, or lectures. May Day was a high point with a parade, speeches, barbecue, and a May pole.

"In cooperative communities dawns are peculiarly rosy," Aldous Huxley wrote with Llano in mind. "For this very reason, mid-day is apt to seem peculiarly stifling, and the afternoons intolerable and interminable."[5] Llano's mid-day was interrupted with continuing factionalism. Harriman was called cunning and evasive, officious and egotistical. He in turn began to feel that no colony could succeed without a prior change in human nature.

Llano's afternoon, however, was haunted by water problems. For effective use of the available water supply, the colony always knew that dams, wells, tunneling, and concrete piping were essential. But the early engineering estimates of underground flow proved faulty, and even for the restricted amount neighboring ranchers disputed the colony's water rights. The worry weighed, and in late 1917 the residents had decreased to two hundred. That fall they heard of twenty thousand acres of pine woods, a sawmill, and a company town near Leesville, Louisiana, available for $120,000. Seizing the opportunity, they arranged a down payment, and Newllano was born. One hundred colonists moved from the Antelope Valley to Louisiana. In one happy period in the late 1920s numbers swelled again to nearly four hundred. The Great Depression, however, intensified all the problems, and Newllano was placed in receivership in 1935. Ten years earlier Harriman, stricken with tuberculosis and suffering from the Louisiana climate, had returned to California. He lived for a few months in Sierra Madre, but died in 1925, fortunately for his spirits well before the demise of his model of economic cooperation.

Gerald Geraldson was a man of Harriman's generation who came near to duplicating his ideological leanings. As a young apprentice carpenter in San Francisco, Bellamy's *Looking Backward* had struck him like fresh wind. In the 1880s he paid dues for several years as a nonresident of the Kaweah commonwealth. He had become the nonviolent socialist who was apt to seek a utopian experiment. His chance came in 1914, the same year Harriman started Llano. By then Geraldson had inherited a one-hundred-acre fruit ranch on the outskirts of Auburn. Most of the socialists thereabout had gone off to join Harriman. Those remaining helped Geraldson start their own group, which they called the Army of Industry. Compared with Llano it was a small experiment, no more than thirty at any one time—the discontented, the jobless, those at odds with the system of private property. In these days before Social Security, the colony was a haven for the poor and unemployed.

For two years they constructed and remodeled buildings for communal use and worked the farm cooperatively. No admission fees were levied, and for a while Geraldson demanded that new members own no property whatever. He held women to be the superior half of society, male domination having come only with the advent of private property. He came to be less and less happy with the fighting and bickering of the men. It takes communal life to penetrate the veneer, he said. He did not lose his faith, though he did come to feel that economic conditions in California were too easy to motivate cooperation. Consequently, he spent much of the rest of his life working in the slums of New York City.

The abolition of private property, at least in the means of production, and the elimination of economic competition— these were almost universal canons in secular utopian experiments. There was, however, a sprinkling of other approaches to the better society. One, for example, was the Little Landers movement led by William E. Smythe. Like John Wesley Powell, the nineteenth-century geologist and explorer, Smythe believed that the future of the West depended on better distribution of

"A little land and a living, surely . . .": Little Landers clubhouse, 1909 (*Courtesy of San Diego Historical Society*)

its available water. He agreed with Henry George that far too much California land was monopolized for speculation, whereas a single acre of irrigated land could provide a living for the average family. He began to lecture on his thesis: "a little land and a living, surely, is better than desperate struggle and wealth, possibly." In 1909 he organized the first Little Landers colony with a dozen families and twenty acres south of San Diego near San Ysidro. By the fourth year 116 families held at least one acre apiece. They marketed their produce cooperatively in San Diego. Their clubhouse, with cobblestone fireplaces, furnished a varied social and intellectual fare, in Smythe's picture comparable to anything a city offered.

Four other Little Landers colonies with from twenty to forty families each were activated—Runnymede near Palo Alto, Hayward Heath across the bay, one near Cupertino, another in the San Fernando Valley. The San Diego colony suffered a disastrous flood, but that was not the only thorn. The five communities slowly disintegrated in the face of two general problems. The amount of land proved inadequate, especially for inexperienced farmers, and the booming job market during World War I tempted and drew off members. Nevertheless, the principle of returning to the soil endured for others.

Fellowship Farm near Puente in 1912 was a similar effort to get city dwellers (in this case from Los Angeles) onto the land while retaining some kind of communal social life. This yearning has been unquenchable in California, at least since the 1870s, and it would see its fullest expression in the rural commune movement of the 1970s. It was often associated with other ideals, as with the younger Theosophists at Halcyon. At Placentia near Anaheim, for example, the Societas Fraternia led by George Hinde and Louis Schlesinger after 1878 combined both a regime of raw food and spiritualism with the growing of prize-winning walnuts, fruit, and vegetables. At Joyful near Bakersfield in the 1880s Isaac Rumford and his followers also added a raw food diet to farming as their key to Eden. At Tuolumne Farms near Modesto in the late 1940s small family farming was combined with pacifism and the dream of a nonmaterialistic as well as a nonmilitaristic society.

These dreams of simplification were based on moralities of the past. Their adherents, like the Little Landers, tended to be older people remembering midwestern farms and one-room schoolhouses. Their leaders were engineers, practical or quiet men, unlike the fiery spirits of Kaweah and Llano. Their fires burned lower than in the socialist colonies, and they compromised with much in the present, though they drew a common line at competition and industrialism. Nostalgia can undergird utopia as effectively as untried aspiration, and its golden age can seem equally distant. The march with loyal comrades shoulder to shoulder to the promised land of yesterday can be as difficult as steps toward a utopian tomorrow.

## CHAPTER SIX

# Modern Communes

CALIFORNIA'S LARGEST and most varied utopian experimentation emerged in the late 1960s. It was associated with the New Left's criticism of an impersonalized, bureaucratic America so glaringly exposed by the Vietnam war. Through the social rifts of these years grew the hopes of a radically reshaped society, usually among the hundreds of young people in the process of abandoning home, college, or city to live communally. Almost overnight the communal dream took the form of a movement. In 1971 David Smith, a physician to San Francisco's Haight-Ashbury district, counted five hundred communes in northern California alone. In them, he estimated, lived ten thousand adults and several hundred children.[1] Sociologists defined these communes as five or more people, most of whom were unrelated by blood or marriage, living together for any reason beyond mere convenience. The utopianism came in their projection of a quality of life seen as substantially different from and superior to what they had known.

Communes were also utopian in their incongruity with surrounding reality. In the nineteenth century, and even until World War II, competition and private property had been the thorns of dissatisfaction. The abolition of these obstacles would call forth an environment of cooperation and sharing that would in turn alleviate human selfishness. The transformation of humanity would arise from a new environment. By the 1960s the perception of the evils in that established world had changed.

Utopians of the Vietnam era were not so sure that the environment was the place to begin. Perhaps an effective change in the society would have to be preceded or at least accompanied by transfigured spiritual and psychological motivations. The watchword became higher consciousness, like the mystical awareness with which Huxley undergirded his unfolding vision in *Island*. Thus David Spangler, resident of various communes in California, discovered the Scottish colony of Findhorn. At this cold North Sea haven, auras of love had transcended rocky soil and harsh storms to produce bounteous flowers and vegetables whose harvest would "merge with an awareness of the greater planet." When Spangler returned to California, he formed the Lorian Association, through which he carried on educational work "oriented to the new age." His purpose was to fight against egotism and visionary impoverishment.[2] Such an attention to individual consciousness did not necessarily jibe with the group orientation of the commune movement. Contradictions were inevitable.

About 1967 individuals seeking the higher consciousness reinvigorated the communal movement. The confluence could be seen following the Summer of Love in San Francisco, where disillusionment with the Haight-Ashbury and the urban counter-culture led a stream of people out to the hinterland of northern California. The inward revolution was still their goal, but now it might come in the context of earth and sky. In that attachment to nature, they were like latter-day romantics, turning their backs on intellect and reason, glorifying youth, and seeking to integrate mind and body and soul.

About this time Lou Gottlieb, a folk musician, threw open the thirty-two acres of his Morning Star Ranch near Occidental to any who wished to live close to the land. By 1967 he and his friend Ramon Sender had attracted over sixty people, and during the following years hundreds wandered through the gate with its carved wooden Indian. Communing with wind and rain, they worked naked in the fields, performed Sioux sun dances, and read Kahlil Gibran by firelight. Work was for those who enjoyed it, a practical recognition that scarcity should no longer be allowed in the industrial world. In an economy of plenty, the proper business of life should not be work but higher thoughts and deeper awareness. For the Gottlieb followers, the path lay through natural foods, a ban on detergents, and ingestions occasionally of LSD. Though they lived communally, the person was the focus and his or her freedom to come and go was important. Unlike most nineteenth-century experiments, the longevity of Morning Star as an institution was never a primary goal.

The ideals of Gottlieb appealed to a young artist and former Yale University student, Bill Wheeler, who had used an inheritance to buy 315 acres of "spacious and lyrical" woods and meadows about eight miles from Morning Star. Wheeler's Ranch or Ahimsa (harmlessness), as it was later called, joined Gottlieb's colony as a mecca for believers in unstructured anarchy, based on the organic order of nature. Here a new breed would bear the message of a social bond stemming from harmony with the natural environment.

Alicia Bay Laurel, a twenty-one-year-old guitarist, was such a seeker after attunement. In 1971 she was living in a hut on Wheeler's land, engaged, as she said, in a love affair with nature. Born Alicia Kaufman with a surgeon father, she had been too restless for college. She hitchhiked across the continent to California, found Wheeler's Ranch, and was fascinated. In residence there, she edited a community news sheet filled with advice on gardening organically, building a simple shelter, making soap from yucca, and birthing babies at home. Eventually she combined the material into a book, *Living on the Earth,* which was published by Random House and sold over a hundred thousand copies. The royalties helped buy groceries for others in the commune.[3]

Wheeler called his ranch "the model of a new age." It would show the compartmentalized, urbanized world a way back to pantheistic anarchism. Cities would be sloughed off like old skins. If the result were a lowering of materialistic living standards, that would mark a positive return to a simpler, voluntary poverty. One method was to divest oneself of the impedimenta of ownership, and to this end Gottlieb tried legally to deed his land to God. Without private property, a sharing, noncompetitive society might be found.

Unquestionably incongruous with the prevailing reality, these two open land communes were predictably subject to hostili-

ties from the outside. One young visitor, Elia Katz, described
Wheeler's place as bleak with roving malcontents, "immense
and irreconcilable angers huddled together."[4] Reflecting even
stronger antipathies, county officials began raids in 1969.
Charges were based on drug usage, fire dangers, and building
code violations. Time after time in the courts the colonists felt
patronized as "smelly savages." Their land was attacked more
directly. By 1973, on sheriff's orders, the temporary dwellings
of both places had been bulldozed to the ground. Even after
that, however, Wheeler was able to maintain a semblance of the
old community at Ahimsa.

Rural communes were, of course, varied in their motivation.
Not all were as incongruous with their surroundings as were the
drug-oriented or anarchistic ones. Sometimes they joined a
major demographic shift away from metropolis and suburb. It
might be noted, however, that the communes' move to the
country imposed a contrasting culture on rural California. Utopians, like Alicia Bay Laurel, were finding mystical overtones in
goats and grains; the products of the land were more than a
farmer's cash crop.

For a group of families who in 1972 acquired forty-eight acres
near Bolinas in Marin County, the land became a prime binding
agent. They named their stream-crossed meadows Paradise Valley and built on it six houses for the families and their eighteen
children. The group included an architect, a tree surgeon, an
illustrator, and a carpenter. For some years they cooperatively
raised a vegetable garden that radiated from a central grassy
plot. Although later the gardens were individualized, the members still considered their life different and better than that of
the urbanized, established world. It was simple in its avoidance
of electricity and running water, and was built on neighborli-
ness, occasional meals together, and weekly or monthly meetings to make the necessary group decisions. Perhaps because
their lifestyle has been less flamboyant, Paradise Valley's bouts
with county officials were far more successful than those at
Morning Star. Paradise Valley was granted variances for com-
post toilets and a five-year extension for bringing their buildings
up to code. The latter assumed that a pioneer farm must devote
its initial energies to the production of food, not housing. One
of the early members felt that Paradise Valley represented a

growing movement leading to a society of small groups living congenially and cooperatively close to the soil.

Paradise Valley and many another rural commune like Yarrow Hill, Happy Valley, or School of the Earth (all near Santa Cruz) or Sunburst Farms (near Santa Barbara) are concerned with survival and the future of human society in a polluted and anxious environment. They withdraw from a competitive, class-ridden economy with the haunting sense that only a simpler life with fewer needs and desires, coupled with the ability to provide food self-sufficiently, may become the only alternative to destruction. In their retreat they seem more like the cooperative utopians of the nineteenth century, but they seldom associate themselves with historic movements. Their rhetoric may suggest pioneers, Indians, or peasant villages, but their eye is on a worrisome future. The process of saving that future involves not just economic self-sufficiency, but smaller, decentralized groups in closer human contact in work, play, education, culture, and spirituality. As one utopian wrote from a wilderness commune, "Get down to the business of creating heaven on earth. Let's affirm our past and say goodbye to it." In the rural environment we may bring our technology up to date with our awareness and discover that in the long run the axe may serve us better than the chain saw.[5]

Ecological concerns are strong in modern utopians and are hardly limited to rural communes. One current of experimentation for a new age is urban as well as ecological. It sees the cities, not abandoned but transformed through extensive home and community gardens, with an emphasis on vegetable rather than animal sources of protein, careful composting and recycling of wastes, changed sources of energy for a simpler life and a cleaner environment.

Camp Joy, a four-acre farm in Boulder Creek near Santa Cruz, is part of a network dedicated to a redirection of urban life. Their gardens and orchards are a model of intensive horticulture, heavy mulching, absence of chemicals, and companion planting for higher yields. Since 1971 the residents have maintained their example of a small farm in an urban context. An idealistic, ecological foundation, the Farallones Institute, has supported them along with other such experiments. One of

Farallones' projects has been Integral House in Berkeley where
an old residence on a fifty-foot lot in a poor section of the city
has been made virtually self-sufficient through rigorous recycling and attention to space.

The anxieties and loneliness of urban life, even without the
ecological strains, have charged the search for closer human ties.
A major component here has been sexual liberation, either in
practices or in attitudes toward sex roles. More open sex, free of
possessiveness, becomes a means of curing society's alienation
and impersonalization. Sex is considered more effective than
economics in energizing the ideal society. Harrad West, in a
large Victorian house on Derby Street in Berkeley, was a community of six adults and two children who experimented for a
year and a half following 1969. It was inspired not only by the
nineteenth-century Oneida Community's complex marriage,
but by the utopian novels of Robert Rimmer in which a small
college called Harrad encouraged direct and open sex. For
Harrad West, group marriage was not promiscuity, requiring instead a sincere commitment of each adult to every member of
the opposite gender. In all their decisions consensus was necessary. Frequent sensitivity sessions were held. In time the de-
manding emotional ties within the group brought several members to change outside jobs to reduce pressure. In the end they
claimed a deepening warmth and understanding: "a larger number of caring persons learning and growing together often can
deal with stresses that can overwhelm two individuals."[6] Although tensions eventually disrupted the group, Hyam Glickman, its eldest member, felt he had been on a social frontier.
The membership was too small and the intensity of the experience too high, exposing as it did the problems each inherited
from the larger society. There was too little economic commitment, he thought; sharing of material resources might have
made a difference. Furthermore, Harrad lacked the spiritual
purpose which Glickman considered to be the heart of the
communities that endured.

Kerista Village, once known as the Purple Submarine, has
grown in San Francisco from three people in 1971 to sixteen in
1980. They live in four Victorian flats near Golden Gate Park,
and are divided into "families" based on polyfidelity, their form

Without jealousy, possessiveness, and anger: Kerista Village, 1980 (*Courtesy of Kerista Village*)

of multiple sexual relationships. They feel they have found a system that successfully eliminates jealousy, possessiveness, and anger. Practicing total income sharing and a growth/communications process called "Gestalt-O-Rama," they seek "the eradication of classism and the obliteration of oppression."[7] With somewhat similar ideals, Stephen Gaskin's Farm, before it moved from its birthplace in California to Tennessee, experimented with nontraditional marriage patterns. A few years after it became rural, however, it reverted to monogamy.

Another more extensive experiment with group marriage, Family Synergy, began in Los Angeles in 1971. Since then, these sympathizers with the basic ideas of Robert Rimmer's novels have revised their scope until now only some forty percent of the members are pursuing group marriage. Most are now concerned with a diversity of life styles, still together hoping for fuller, more rewarding lives as "a supportive community of friends" interested in open of multilateral marriages. They have organized at least four communal houses in the Los Angeles area, and claim six hundred California members with smaller chapters in northern California, a testimonial to "the warm ambiance of Family Synergy or the anomie of life in Los Angeles, or both."[8]

The strains of urban life inevitably kindle dreams of a better way. San Francisco's Black Bart center from 1972 to 1978 expressed these underlying dissatisfactions and potential directions. It focused not on young rebels, but on those over thirty, reasonably well established in job and society, but feeling their lives routine, materialistic, dessicated, and meaningless. They were encouraged to become "middle age dropouts," starting over again with changed life styles and work related to their deeper purposes. As Lou Durham, a minister and founder, put it, their direction lay "away from the dehumanizing effects of mass systems." One of its associated work cooperatives, Briarpatch, used the slogan "living joyfully between the cracks." Life should be simplified, integrated, cooperative, fulfilling, worthwhile, as a result of this "community that you carry around in your mind." To this end they conducted job counseling, a "skills bank" for work exchanges, and weekly Black Bart "rap sessions," and associated themselves with several communal houses. This supportive system also included a journal, *The Black Bart Brigade,* published by Irving Thomas, called a guru of the center. Betty Romanoff, a four-year member, felt the whole scheme was so realistic that it should not be considered utopian, but she admitted that most members believed their program might some day lead to a radically changed society.[9]

The number of communal houses in the San Francisco Bay area grew from an estimated ten in 1973 to more than sixty by 1978. They usually include about six adults and a few children and conceive of themselves as initiating a substantially changed, cooperative way. At San Jose House in San Francisco or Harwood House in Oakland, for example, members hold outside jobs, often professional, but come together evenings and weekends for meals, recreation, and companionship. If there are personal conflicts, they are seen as better than isolation. After house meetings, one member, Melvin Gurtov, felt "cleansed and content," with a stronger individuality. He would contend that the prime ideal of the communal house is the flowering of the human potential in contrast to the largely monotonous, stultifying lives in the established society.[10]

Communal arrangements have been used by a variety of urban movements, like Morehouse and Synanon. Victor Barranco, a former real-estate promoter, incorporated Morehouse in 1969 for "the educational and scientific pursuit and development of the human mind."[11] By 1972 there were ten Morehouses, mostly in the San Francisco Bay area, but also a few in Los Angeles, San Diego, and Hawaii. Escaping the lovelessness and drift of the outside world, they came together to emphasize the positive and contend that anyone could have and do whatever he or she wanted. The process was aided by long sensitivity sessions called Mark Groups, and members took classes through the Institute of Human Abilities. In 1977 the communal houses were deemphasized; all but one of them closed, and the organization continued as More University with about eighty fulltime students at its campus in Lafayette. Synanon, although its roots were very different and concerned with drug rehabilitation, had transformed itself by the early 1970s into a communal answer to urban life. Actually it used a technique, The Game, that was similar to the Mark Group of Morehouse. Both explored human identity and hoped to reshape attitudes for a cooperative, loving, communal experience.

Project One, in a five-story warehouse on Howard Street near San Francisco's Mission district, answered urban discontent in a different way. In 1969 a few artists seeking space at a reasonable rate proposed to lease the 80,000 square feet of the abandoned building, and when they advertised for recruits were amazed at the turnout of over four hundred allies. Subsequently the raw space was partitioned into units for over a hundred people living communally and working collectively. The immense structure in its heyday included a child-care center and schools, studios, offices, a "people's computer," and a communal kitchen. With changes in organization through the years, the building in 1979 housed about fifty people generally committed to a cooperative life and to the sharing of resources and skills. At that time the owners initiated eviction proceedings and on August 1, 1980, sheriff's deputies in jumpsuits and carrying batons swept the handful of remaining residents from the scene.[12]

Harvey Cox has seen the rebirth in our day of the monastic utopian tradition, the creation of religious models like seed

Communal life in Project One, San Francisco, 1980 (*Courtesy of Craig Baldwin*)

plots for the rest of society.[13] Certainly the religious commune would confirm that assessment, and in California those turning to eastern religions are as noticeable as those carrying on the collective ideas of Christianity. Religious communes do not proclaim political revolution but rather spiritual change, and so they stand with the utopianism that works through the individual not the social environment. Their orientation, as it had in the past, continued to be inward and upward more than outward.

Paramahansa Yogananda, whose activities were discussed in a previous chapter, once said that cooperative colonies, signs of the new age, would "spread through the world like wildfire." More than any other of Yogananda's disciples, James Donald Walters, who was given the name Kriyananda, implemented those expectations. Kriyananda, educated at Kent School, Haverford, and Brown, as a young seeker had found the writings of Yogananda in a New York bookstore and almost immediately crossed the continent to Encinitas to find his Master. Much later, in 1967, long after Yogananda's death, Kriyananda was able to initiate his communitarian ideals when he bought seventy-two acres covered with pines and oaks in the Sierra foothills near Nevada City. He had found the land through a chance meeting with Richard Baker of the Zen Center in San Francisco. Baker was at that time searching for a location for his future retreat, Tassajara. Though the two purchased adjacent land near Nevada City, it was Kriyananda who soon declared it his spiritual home and in 1968 opened Ananda. By then several geodesic domes had risen among the manzanita, architecturally lowering the bowl of heaven to an energy field commensurate with the human skull.

A cooperative colony was the next step. Six miles down the road rose the farm or Ananda Cooperative Village. The first families arrived in 1969. At any given time up to one hundred and sixty people live there. They prohibit drugs and alcohol, and each member, including Kriyananda, has only one vote. The colony has survived two disastrous fires and hopes soon to retire its mortgage. Kriyananda continues to claim that personal transformation is "the key to social change." "We find our peace inwardly first in meditation," he says, "and only secondarily from one another." That inner peace will keep running smoothly the machinery of the new age.[14]

Ananda has been the most evident, but there have been other communal expressions in connection with Eastern religious retreats. Tassajara, for example, established its thriving Zen mountain center east of Monterey, where Richard Baker turned after leaving Kriyananda's Nevada City area in 1967. To feed those at Tassajara and at the headquarters in San Francisco, these Buddhists constructed a separate communal farm in 1972 called Green Gulch near Muir Beach in Marin County. Here thirty to forty people continue to grow organic vegetables and study Zen philosophy in a quiet dedication to harmony and discipline.

Western Christianity has spawned an even greater number of experiments on countless city streets and country roads. One example from the late 1960s was led by Jack Sparks under the name Christian World Liberation Front. Sparks, a former Campus Crusader, and his followers set up a communal house on Dwight Way in Berkeley and at the same time supported a rural commune, the Rising Sun, in Humboldt County. They published a newspaper, *Right On,* and specialized in street theater.

The millennium and the Age of Aquarius are one, they said, "moving toward some dimly sensed crossing point," the global unification of mankind.[15]

At Lighthouse Ranch on a bluff twelve miles south of Eureka, sixty to one hundred fifty Christians of the Gospel Outreach have lived communally since 1970. James Durkin, a less-than-successful realtor in Eureka, brought them together as part of his own spiritual search. They hoped to live "wholly and completely" for God, achieving integrated lives based on a mission, spreading Christian love by living in community and sharing possessions. At Lighthouse and nearby they run a farm with cows and chickens, a food store, a restaurant, an advertising sheet, and various small businesses. Eventually they seek to reach people everywhere, "from every segment of society: young, aged, crippled, blind, rich, middle-class, poor, black, yellow, white—every person."[16] Their teams have formed satellite houses in Whittier, Perris, San Diego, and San Francisco as well as outside the state. Such an outreach is nothing new for Christianity, of course; it is the essence of traditional evangelism. Yet through the life of men like Jim Durkin the thrust is also a clue to the conception of California as a special place on the earth's surface, where both the state and the people enjoy a unique destiny.

These descriptions of specific communes, secular or religious, obscure the serial or dynamic nature of modern utopianism. Individuals move from group to group, and the communes themselves expect minimal stability or continuity. In this sense they unconsciously conform to the American acquiescence in rapid change. Of course, the modern movement has itself evolved: the hippie-drug communes of the 1960s merged into the rural escapes of the early 1970s or into the personal growth and alternative life styles later in the decade. A few years were considered a reasonable organizational life span, and within that time members were expected to come and go according to their personal needs.

The migrants, however, seldom let the demise of a colony scuttle their dream of the cooperative way. Like letters recombining in an anagram, successive expressions recast the basic meanings. Harrad West, for instance, may have died, but five of its members still feel like an extended family, and one of them, Hyam Glickman, hoped some day to start Oneida Three in which he would weave economic sharing into the Harrad sexual ideals. Black Bart's former people have moved on to other forms of communal housing or collectives. When the institutions remain vital, as with Project One or Camp Joy, the membership nevertheless comes and goes in cycles.

As a consequence, California utopianism seems caught in an underlying restlessness. Though its values—sharing, cooperation, simplicity—remain constant, its institutions do not. Perhaps because its visionaries have been heirs of middle-class prosperity, facing a wealth of possibilities, their propensity toward movement may reflect the multitude of choices. Michael Medved described his southern California high school class of 1965 as one confronting unprecedented alternatives in careers, love, living arrangements, and basic values. "With so many options to consider, was it any wonder that we had such a difficult time making up our minds?"[17]

By the late 1970s, secular utopia became quieter, less raucous, less willing to proclaim certainty. The result may have derived from its nonauthoritarian effort, its deliberate desire to eliminate the will to power. Achievement, goals, and success were less often esteemed. Faith in institutions was eroded, especially in the rigidity and dehumanizing materialism of industrial organization. Instead, utopians talked of silent pulses, or muted drums, rhythms ultimately connected with all other rhythms, throbbing outward to encompass the universe.

Robert Owen in the 1820s envisaged his New Harmony as a vast network of cooperating communities. That network ideal is very much alive in the California vision. From 1971 to 1976, for example, the Albion Community Center enacted what Nicole Ginsberg, a former New York YMCA worker, called her "fantasizing" on an ideal community. In the area south of Mendocino, the center she helped build served a web of communes and other groups in the cooperative purchase of food, and provided a small restaurant, a used-clothing exchange, a nursery school, a library, and a general gathering place for weddings, dances, and recreation.[18] Vocations for Social Change in Oakland during the mid-1970s and New Directions in San Francisco later in the decade coordinated a variety of utopian schemes. Likewise,

Well Being in 1971 began in San Anselmo as a network of communal living but changed its focus to spiritual communality, continuing in that vein till the present. Journals like the *Modern Utopian* (1967–1972), *Kaliflower* (1969–1972), *Communities* (1972–present), *Common Ground* (1974–present), and the *Whole Person Catalogue* (1977–present), to mention a few, have tried to hold various strands together. One such, *Grapevine,* itself run by a collective, covers the joys, problems, and skills of group living.

These communal networks have not yet noticeably broadened the base of their utopian clientele. Organized labor and Marxist radical networks, which might be thought congenial, now overlap but little. In California's past both workers and Marxists were intimately involved with the communitarian venture. The Marxists retired, however, after their break with the Socialist Party in 1917; organized labor, after its victories in the New Deal. So communitarianism became an arena for the middle class which, it might be remembered, has been the seedbed of most modern revolutions.

The radical and labor contingents had come to see communitarianism as too chimerical, too doused with whimsy and fantasy. The later California experience often bore them out. In the past, the California utopian had redefined whole environments, transposed Mediterranean views, and thought of staircases sweeping to the sea. The modern counterpart made similar leaps while imagining other environmental redefinitions like Callenbach's *Ecotopia.* Sometimes the contemporary reveled in mystical kingdoms like that of Tolkien's *Lord of the Rings* where no shadow lay and life was lived as if it were inside a song. Then he named his commune House of the Seventh Angel, Magic Forest, Never Land, Mu Family, Zanadu, Rivendell, or Lorien.

No matter how restricted or inconstant its modern constituency, utopia remains a serious commentary on its surroundings. It continues, for example, to emerge from disillusion, and in contemplating the prevailing society occasionally sinks to prognostications of doom. Kriyananda considers "the impending cataclysm" a prime motive in founding his community, and Ananda sees its cooperative vision partly as preparation for disaster. Black Bart offered survival in a threatened world. Harrad West began with fundamental disenchantment with monogamy and society. The Christian World Liberation Front spoke of "this ugly, insane, and impossible cycle about to be played all over again—for the last time." The utopian answers have been propitiations of the future to avoid the pain of the present. As such, they offer surcease from the bitterness and cynicism of their time through the unifying communal vision of an ideal society.

# The Unclouded Horizon

THE COMPLEXITY and gestalt of a region like California can never be understood through only one of its ideas or groups. Any explanation, as Joan Didion found, "flickers on the horizon, ever receding, ever diminishing."[1] In that fitful way, utopianism must throw a partial light. Close around each utopian idea stand its contraries. Opposite Helena Modjeska's friends and dreamers worked the square-toed German farmers planting their colony at Anaheim. Beside Henry George was Ambrose Bierce, cynically defining hope as no more than a clerkship in the United States mint, or feeling, as Graham Greene once put it, that heaven should remain where it belonged—on the other side of death. In the same state with the visionaries of Big Sur describing the world as an air-conditioned nightmare reside people incapable of imagining any place better than Orange County. Along with the expansive buoyancy of Abbott Kinney have grown fears of cultural deprivation, as expressed by James Phelan, or aching identifications of destitution, as felt by Tom Mooney. The romantic myth created by Hollywood called forth a response in authors like Nathanael West, who wrote "out of frustration and betrayed hopes about a landscape of endless magnitude but without center or coherence and in which the past existed only in movie lot falsifications and architectural charades."[2]

The utopian, however, is never far removed from his cynical opposite. Both have been saddened by contemplating the pastoral Eden that might have been and disillusioned by the unequal distribution of abundance. But the utopian has gone on to visions and experiments with substantial change. A new age might come through economics as with Henry George, through politics as with Upton Sinclair, through the arts as with Henry Miller, through a religious awakening as with Katherine Tingley, through a socialistic model as with Job Harriman, or through a small commune as with Lou Gottlieb. Sometimes the dreamer withdrew, sometimes burrowed from within, but in California he always manifested "an awareness of the significance of this great moment of human transition."[3]

The impelling causes, the aspects of the prevailing society most repellent to the utopian, have been individualistic competition based upon private profit, the materialistic worship of growth, urban loneliness, and the warring environments of class versus class. In their place the utopian would propose a decentralized marketplace, cooperative sharing, an equalitarian society of fulfilling work, integrated lives, and simple joys. The dream suggested the theosophical vision of a new race rising on Pacific shores, but more importantly it was revolutionary prophecy, the bold, motivating ideas necessary for effective social change.

A critic of Hermann Hesse once wrote, "It is terrifying and very dangerous to be too right and too soon about anything fundamental."[4] The utopian is often trapped in that situation. But, alas, he is sometimes wrong and out of phase, as witness a Charles Manson or a Jim Jones. The difference between a prophet and a crank lies in the context of the prophet's values, in his willingness to chart a new course based on ideals as old as love and brotherhood. His virtue rises from the courage or the ability to see the old anew. As Aldous Huxley said, "It is not at the center, not from within the organization, that the saint can cure our regimented insanity; it is only from without, at the periphery."[5]

Such values, like perfection, can be fraught with danger, leading to unrealistic expectations and failure to allow for slow maturation. Perhaps that is why, when they end in tyranny, the best of revolutions are thought to have begun in the wrong. Of course, even at the outset, the illusions of utopia can be signs of mental illness and pathological failure to address reality. But illusions can as well be therapeutic and creative. Once again, it is the application of values to the perceived reality that makes the difference.

Compare two Californians and their utopianism, separated by over a century. Lansford Hastings in 1846 viewed California as "one grand scene of continued improvement."[6] If there were values in his thinking, they were no more than an indiscriminate attraction to growth and material prosperity without concern for the quality of that growth or the consequences of prosperity to the region. He was the forerunner of countless boomers and developers.

Herbert Marcuse, the late Marxian philosopher who taught during his latter years at the University of California, San Diego, talked in 1969 of utopia in a completely different way. "The world of human freedom," he said, "cannot be built by established societies."[7] The complacency of suburbia can never bring about a global abolition of poverty. Modes of behavior arising solely from a familiar abundance will not lead to a deepening of sensibilities, new theoretical considerations, or any substantial change. The only hope is to break into another consciousness, and here Marcuse turned toward utopia for the daring thinkers who would become the vanguards. In the late 1960s the bearers of that utopianism and of his hopes certainly included the communitarian idealists of the time. The communards, however, were heirs of the affluent middle class. Ironically for Marcuse, they should have yielded no more than social sterility or, at best, the boomer utopianism of a Hastings. Yet they had transcended their class to foresee radical reformations. Their values had triumphed over their economic backgrounds. In this sense they stood as prophets, not cranks. Of course, the full impact of their behavior cannot yet be measured, and they may eventually sink back into complacency. But even if that happens, judging from California's past, we can assume that others will arise, perhaps too soon, too right, but always ready and waiting "with laughter and attunement [to] free the splendor of the new culture that is emerging."[8]

# NOTES

## PREFACE

1. Henry George, *Progress and Poverty* (1879; New York: Robert Schalkenbach Foundation, 1962), 464.

2. As quoted in Emmett Greenwalt, *The Point Loma Community in California, 1897–1942* (Berkeley: University of California Press, 1955), 19.

## CHAPTER ONE

1. Joan Didion, *Slouching towards Bethlehem* (New York: Dell, 1968), 172; Ernest Callenbach, *Ecotopia: The Notebooks and Reports of William Weston* (New York: Bantam, 1975), 5–7, 16, 22, 24, 43–46.

2. George W. James, *California: Romantic and Beautiful* (Boston: Page Co., 1914), 119–120.

3. James Q. Wilson, "A Guide to Reagan Country: The Political Culture of Southern California," *Commentary*, XLIII (May 1967), 41.

4. Horace Bell, *Reminiscences of a Ranger* (1881; Santa Barbara: Wallace Hebberd, 1927), 439–442.

5. Josiah Royce, *California: From the Conquest in 1846 to the Second Vigilance Committee in San Francisco—A Study of American Character* (New York: Alfred A. Knopf, 1948), 57.

6. Melvin Lasky, *Utopia and Revolution: On the Origins of a Metaphor* (Chicago: University of Chicago Press, 1976), 15.

7. Royce, *California*, 26; Royce, *Race Questions, Provincialism, and Other American Problems* (New York: Macmillan, 1908), 88; Peter Fuss, *The Moral Philosophy of Josiah Royce* (Cambridge, Mass.: Harvard University Press, 1965), 233.

## CHAPTER TWO

1. Lewis Mumford, *The Story of Utopias* (reprint; Gloucester, Mass.: Peter Smith, 1959), 297.

2. Bret Harte, "The Right Eye of the Commander," in *The Outcasts of Poker Flat and Other Tales* (reprint; New York: New American Library, 1961), 17.

3. Jack London, *Burning Daylight* (New York: Arcadia House, 1950), 68; London, *Valley of the Moon* (New York: Macmillan, 1916), 87–88, 254, 271.

4. Theodore S. Van Dyke, *Southern California* (New York: Fords, Howard, and Hulbert, 1886), 88; Van Dyke, *Millionaires of a Day* (1890; Louisville, Ky.: Lost Cause Press, 1968), 208.

5. Helena Modjeska, *Memories and Impressions* (New York: Macmillan, 1910), 251, 252.

6. Franklin Walker, *Seacoast of Bohemia* (reprint, Santa Barbara: Peregrine Smith, 1973), 11, 59; Lawrence Clark Powell, *Robinson Jeffers* (Pasadena: San Pasqual Press, 1940), 15; Robinson Jeffers, *Californians* (New York: Cayucos Books, 1971), 131, 133.

7. Henry Miller *Big Sur and the Oranges of Hieronymus Bosch* (New York: New Directions Books, 1957), 6, 34, 403.

8. Aldous Huxley, *After Many a Summer* (London: Chatto & Windus, 1950), 242–245; *Brave New World* (New York: Harper & Bros., 1946), x–xii; *Ape and Essence* (New York: Harper & Bros., 1948), 125–126; *Island* (New York: Harper & Row, 1962); Charles M. Holmes, *Aldous Huxley and the Way to Reality* (Bloomington: Indiana University Press, 1970), p. xiii; Hal Bridges, *American Mysticism: From William James to Zen* (New York: Harper & Row, 1970), 87.

9. Tom Wolfe, *The Electric Kool-Aid Acid Test* (New York: Farrar, Straus & Giroux, 1968), 26, 27, 61.

10. George Slusser, review of Darko Suvin, *Metamorphoses of Science Fiction*, in *Nineteenth Century Fiction*, XXXV (June 1980), 74.

## CHAPTER THREE

1. Thomas S. Hines, *Burnham of Chicago: Architect and Planner* (New York: Oxford University Press, 1974), 180; see also Judd Kahn, *Imperial San Francisco* (Lincoln: University of Nebraska Press, 1979).

2. Lawrence Lipton, *The Holy Barbarians* (New York: Julian Messner, 1959), 15, 17, 295; Reyner Banham, *Los Angeles: The Architecture of Four Ecologies* (Harmondsworth, England: Penguin, 1976), 160.

3. Harvey Cox, *The Feast of Fools: A Theological Essay on Festivity and Fantasy* (Cambridge, Mass.: Harvard University Press, 1969), 82.

4. Nathanael West, *The Day of the Locust* (1939; New York: Farrar, Straus, Cudahy, 1957), 262.

5. Banham, *Los Angeles*, 124; for Disneyland, see Mark Gottdiener, "Disneyland: A Utopian Urban Space" (ms. in possession of author, 1980), 1–11.

6. Charles Albro Barker, *Henry George* (New York: Oxford University Press, 1955), 265–266.

7. Henry George, *Progress and Poverty* (1879; New York: Robert Schalkenback Foundation, 1962), 405, 405–407, 421.

8. Albert Fried, *Socialism in America: From the Shakers to the Third International* (Garden City, N.Y.: Doubleday, 1970), 470; John Steinbeck, *In Dubious Battle* (New York: Random House, 1936), 200.

9. Melvyn Dubofsky, *We Shall Be All: A History of the Industrial Workers of the World* (Chicago: Quadrangle Books, 1969), 155; Industrial Workers of the World, *Songs of the Workers: On the Road, in the Jungles and in the Shops* (Spokane, Wash.: Spokane Local of the IWW, n.d.), 22, 26.

10. Francis E. Townsend, *New Horizons* (Chicago: J. L. Stewart, 1943), 177.

11. Warren W. Wagar, "The Steel-Gray Saviour: Technocracy as Utopia and Ideology," *Alternative Futures*, II (Spring 1979), 39.

12. Upton Sinclair, "I, Governor of California and How I Ended Poverty: A True Story of the Future" (Los Angeles: Upton Sinclair, 1933), 14, 15.

## CHAPTER FOUR

1. Carey McWilliams, *Southern California Country* (New York: Duell, Sloan, Pearce, 1946), 249.

2. Curt Gentry, *Last Days of the Late, Great State of California* (New York: Putnam, 1968), 13.

3. As quoted in Kevin Starr, *Americans and the California Dream, 1850–1915* (New York: Oxford University Press, 1973), 99.

4. Edward O. C. Ord, *The City of Angels and the City of Saints* (San Marino: Huntington Library, 1978), 35.

5. As quoted in Robert V. Hine, *California's Utopian Colonies* (reprint, New Haven, Conn.: Yale University Press, 1966), 29. In this chapter all quotations, unless otherwise noted, are taken from this work.

6. Vincent Bugliosi, *Helter Skelter* (New York: Norton, 1974), 415.

7. Hine, *Colonies,* 43.

8. *Temple Artisan,* LII (February–March 1952), 68; (August–September 1951), 16; (October–November 1951), 37; Harold Forgostein to Robert Hine, July 18, 1979.

9. Robert V. Hine, "Cult and Occult in California," *Pacific Spectator,* VIII (Summer 1954), 198–200.

10. Harvey Cox, *Turning East* (New York: Simon & Schuster, 1977), 93, 96; for a fuller discussion of emergent religions, including the I Am movement of the previous paragraph, see Robert Ellwood, Jr., *Alternative Altars: Unconventional and Eastern Spirituality in America* (Chicago: University of Chicago Press, 1979), chap. 3.

11. Hine, *Colonies,* 103.

12. Paul Kagan, *New World Utopias* (New York: Penguin Books, 1975), 138–157.

## CHAPTER FIVE

1. Aldous Huxley, "Ozymandias, the Utopia that Failed," in *Tomorrow and Tomorrow and Tomorrow* (New York: Harpers, 1956), 89.

2. As quoted in Robert V. Hine, *California's Utopian Colonies* (reprint, New Haven, Conn.: Yale University Press, 1966), 68; in this chapter all quotations, unless otherwise noted, are taken from this work.

3. Dolores Hayden, *Seven American Utopias: The Architecture of Communitarian Socialism* (Cambridge, Mass.: MIT Press, 1976), 300–302.

4. Knox Mellon, "Job Harriman and the Politics of Utopia," paper presented at Pacific Coast Branch of the American Historical Association, San Diego, August 19, 1976), 7.

5. Huxley, *Tomorrow,* 89.

## CHAPTER SIX

1. Riverside *Press,* May 26, 1971.

2. Paul Hawken, *The Magic of Findhorn* (New York: Bantam Books, 1976), 290–297.

3. *New York Times,* March 26, 1971; Ramon Sender and Bill Wheeler,

eds., "Home Free: A History of Morning Star Ranch and Wheeler's Ahimsa" (typescript, 1978; Special Collections, Library, University of California, Riverside), 160–162.

4. Elia Katz, *Armed Love* (New York: Holt, Rinehart & Winston, 1971), 173.

5. Paul Williams, *Das Energi* (New York: Warner Books, 1973), 15, 136.

6. Harrad West, "Statement of Purpose" (ms. in author's possession); interview with Hyam Glickman, August 16 and 19, 1974.

7. Purple Submarine (Kerista), "Statement of Purpose" (ms. in author's possession); interviews with Eve Furchgott, August 2, 1974, and December 27, 1979.

8. Hy Levy, "Family Synergy, *Communities,* XXXXI (December–January 1979–80), 25.

9. Interviews with Lou Durham, Ron Steingold, Betty Romanoff, and Hal Howard, August 1974 and December 1979.

10. Melvin Gurtov, *Making Changes: The Politics of Self Liberation* (Oakland, Calif.: Harvest Moon Books, 1979), 194. For the number of communal houses, see "House Directory," in *Oakland Grapevine,* December 1979; Eric Raimy, *Shared Houses, Shared Lives: The New Extended Families and How They Work* (Los Angeles: J. P. Tarcher, 1979). For a movement calling for communal houses for the elderly, see *Los Angeles Times,* Feb. 7, 1980.

11. David Felton, ed., *Mindfuckers* (San Francisco: Straight Arrow Books, 1972), 110; *Wall Street Journal,* April 9, 1974, 1–2, 19.

12. Judson Jerome, *Families of Eden* (New York: Seabury Press, 1974), 105–119; *San Francisco Examiner,* August 1, 1980.

13. Harvey Cox, *The Feast of Fools: A Theological Essay on Festivity and Fantasy* (Cambridge, Mass.: Harvard University Press, 1969), 90.

14. Donald Walters (Kriyananda), *The Path* (Nevada City, Calif.: Ananda Publications, 1977), 6–166, 612–613; *Los Angeles Times,* July 16, 1972. Likewise Eastern, the Lama Foundation attracted a large number of Californians to the solitudes near Taos, New Mexico, following 1966. Since the late 1960s, the Hare Krishna movement and the Universal Church of the Reverend Sun Myung Moon have maintained communal living situations, both in urban centers like Los Angeles and in outlying areas like Aetna Springs near St. Helena. Neither of these cults, however, in origin or development can be claimed as peculiarly Californian.

**15.** *Right On* (July–August 1974). Koinonia in Santa Cruz in the early 1970s ran a large restaurant as an adjunct to its Christian cooperative living.

**16.** "Lighthouse Ranch," *Communities,* No. 13 (March–April, 1975), 48; *Gospel Outreach* (Eureka, Calif.: Radiance Publications, 1978).

**17.** Michael Medved and David Wallchinsky, *What Really Happened to the Class of '65?* (New York: Random House, 1976), 144.

**18.** Interview with Nicole Ginsberg by Linda Wickert, December 15, 1979; typescript in Mendocino County Museum, Willits, Calif.

## AFTERWORD

**1.** Joan Didion, *Slouching towards Bethlehem* (New York: Dell Publications, 1961), 121.

**2.** Karl Lamb, *As Orange Goes* (New York: W. W. Norton, 1974), 179; David Fine, "California as Dystopia," *Alternative Futures,* II (Fall 1979), 30.

**3.** R. Buckminster Fuller, *Utopia or Oblivion: The Prospects for Humanity* (New York: Bantam Books, 1969), 340.

**4.** Review of Edgar Friedenberg, *Harpers,* CCXLV (July 1972), 88.

**5.** Aldous Huxley, *Ape and Essence* (New York: Harper & Bros., 1948), 8.

**6.** Lansford Hastings, *The Emigrants' Guide to Oregon and California* (1845; Princeton, N.J.: Princeton University Press, 1932), 151.

**7.** Herbert Marcuse, *An Essay on Liberation* (Boston: Beacon Press, 1969), 6.

**8.** Herbert Marcuse, *Statement of Purpose* (Lorian Assn., Elgin, Ill., 1980), 1.

# BIBLIOGRAPHY

## General

The cultural history of California that deals most fully with utopianism is Kevin Starr, *Americans and the California Dream, 1850–1915* (New York: Oxford University Press, 1973). Joan Didion, *Slouching towards Bethlehem* (New York: Dell, 1968), and James Wilson, "A Guide to Reagan Country: The Political Culture of Southern California," *Commentary,* XLIII (May 1967), 37–45, are more personalized views.

Two recent works are important for definitions: Melvin Lasky, *Utopia and Revolution: On the Origins of a Metaphor* (Chicago: University of Chicago Press, 1976); and Frank and Fritzie Manuel, *Utopian Thought in the Western World* (Cambridge, Mass.: Harvard University Press, 1979). The earlier Lewis Mumford, *The Story of Utopias* (reprint, Gloucester, Mass.: Peter Smith, 1959) is opinionated but still useful. Extremely useful is Robert Fogarty, *Dictionary of American Communal and Utopian History* (Westport, Conn.: Greenwood, 1980).

## Literature

In addition to the works of and by the authors mentioned in Chapter One, see Franklin Walker, *Literary History of Southern California* (Berkeley: University of California Press, 1950), and *Seacoast of Bohemia* (Santa Barbara: Peregrine Smith, 1973). A classic example of modern utopian literature is Ernest Callenbach, *Ecotopia: The Notebooks and Reports of William Weston* (New York: Bantam, 1975).

## Politics and Economics

For the best biography of the pioneer economist, see Charles Barker, *Henry George* (New York: Oxford, 1955). A good background for Upton Sinclair is Robert Burke, *Olson's New Deal for California* (Berkeley: University of California Press, 1953). Carey McWilliams, *Southern California Country: An Island on the Land* (New York: Duell, Sloan, and Pearce, 1946) is full of insights. For movements like technocracy, see Luther Whiteman and Samuel Lewis, *Glory Roads: The Psychological State of California* (New York: Crowell, 1936). For architecture, see David Gebhard and Robert Winter, *A Guide to Architecture in Southern California* (Los Angeles: Los Angeles County Museum of Art, 1955), and *A Guide to Architecture in San Francisco and Northern California* (Santa Barbara: Peregrine Smith, 1973); and Reyner Banham, *Los Angeles: The Architecture of Four Ecologies* (Harmondsworth, Eng.: Penguin, 1971).

# Religion

Studies of recent religious movements are Robert Ellwood, Jr., *Alternative Altars: Unconventional and Eastern Spirituality in America* (Chicago: University of Chicago Press, 1979); Harvey Cox, *Turning East: The Promise and Peril of the New Orientalism* (New York: Simon & Schuster, 1977); and Jacob Needleman, *The New Religions* (New York: Doubleday, 1971). Good insights, especially in connection with Theosophy, are in Laurence Veysey, *The Communal Experience: Anarchist and Mystical Counter-Cultures in America* (New York: Harper & Row, 1973). David St. Clair, *The Psychic World of California* (New York: Doubleday, 1972), is more specific. More generally interpretative are Charles Glock and Robert Bellah, eds., *The New Religious Consciousness* (Berkeley: University of California Press, 1976); and Robert Withnow, *The Consciousness Reformation* (Berkeley: University of California Press, 1976).

# Experimental Colonies

For the story to World War I, see Robert Hine, *California's Utopian Colonies* (New York: Norton, 1966). More recent treatments which include California are Robert Fogarty, *American Utopianism* (Itasca, Ill.: Peacock, 1972), Dolores Hayden, *Seven*

*American Utopias: The Architecture of Communitarian Socialism* (Cambridge, Mass.: MIT Press, 1976); Paul Kagan, *New World Utopias* (New York: Penguin, 1975); and Ron Roberts, *The New Communes: Coming Together in America* (Englewood Cliffs, N.J.: Prentice-Hall, 1971). A few California colonies are decried in Elia Katz, *Armed Love* (New York: Holt, 1971) and extolled in Robert Houriet, *Getting Back Together* (New York: Avon, 1971). Three sociological analyses embracing a few California movements are Rosabeth Kanter, *Commitment and Community: Communes and Utopias in Sociological Perspective* (Cambridge, Mass.: Harvard University Press, 1972); Hugh Gardner, *Children of Prosperity: Thirteen Modern American Communes* (New York: St. Martin's Press, 1978); and Benjamin Zablocki, *Alienation and Charisma* (New York: Free Press, 1980).

# INDEX